The Ali Abbas Story

The Ali Abbas Story

JANE WARREN

HarperCollins*Entertainment*
An Imprint of HarperCollins*Publishers*

HarperCollins*Publishers*
77–85 Fulham Palace Road,
Hammersmith, London W6 8JB

www.harpercollins.co.uk

Published by HarperCollins*Publishers* 2004
1 3 5 7 9 8 6 4 2

A catalogue record for this book
is available from the British Library

ISBN 0 00 718113 2

Set in Sabon

Printed and bound in Great Britain by
Clays Ltd, St Ives plc

This book is dedicated to an honourable man,
Mohammed Abd Hamza Al-Sultani,
who has given Ali a new beginning.

HarperCollins*Publishers* would like to thank the
following for providing photographs and for
permission to reproduce copyright material.

*While every effort has been made to trace the owners of
copyright material reproduced herein, the publishers would
like to apologise for any omissions and will be pleased to
incorporate missing acknowledgements in any future editions.*

Page 2 *top right and lower photos*
© Stewart Innes and Peter Wilson
Page 3 *top photo* © Mirrorpix
Page 4 *top photo* © Roger Corke;
lower photo © Roger Corke
Page 5 *top photo* © Getty Images
Page 6 *top photo* © Getty Images;
middle and lower photos © PA Photos
Page 7 *photos* © Diana Morgan
Page 8 *top photo* © Corbis;
lower photo © Kuwaiti Ministry of Health
Education and Media Department

Contents

The ultimate measure of a man is not where he stands in moments of comfort and convenience, but where he stands at times of challenge and controversy.

Martin Luther King

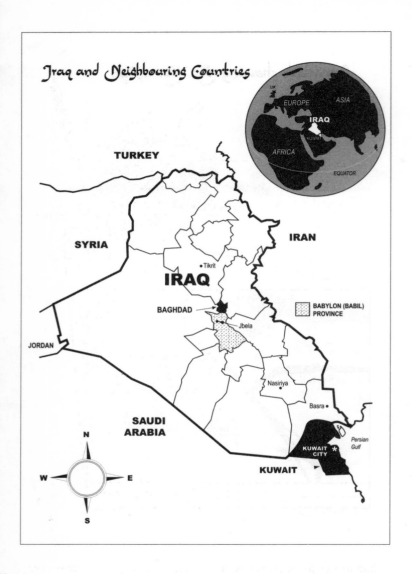

Iraq and Neighbouring Countries

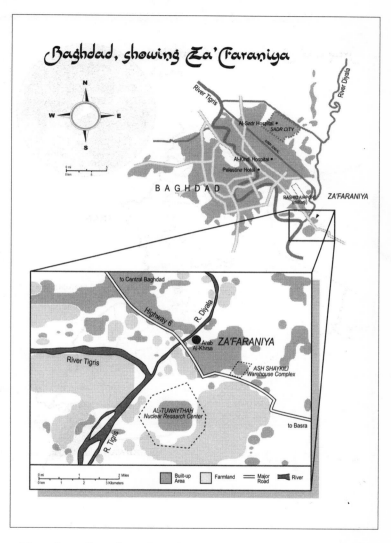

Map of significant locations in Baghdad, including Ali's home – the Arab Al-Khrsa – and the two hospitals where he was treated.

xi

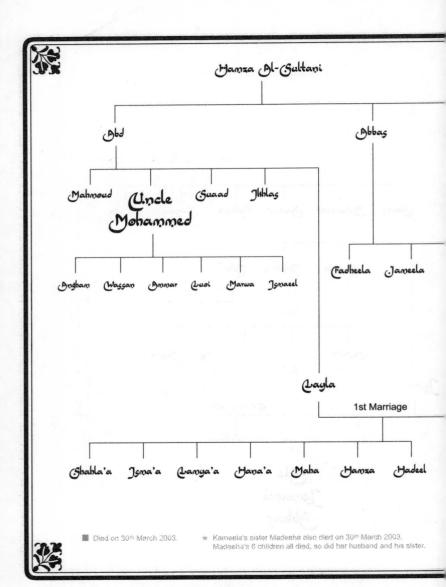

Ali's family tree

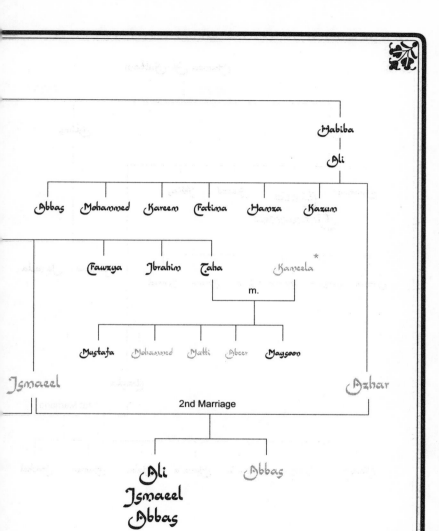

Habiba

Ali

Abbas Mohammed Kareem Fatima Hamza Kazum

Fawzya Ibrahim Taha Kameela *

m.

Mustafa Mohammed Malki Abeer Maysoon

Ismaeel Azhar

2nd Marriage

Ali
Ismaeel
Abbas

Abbas

ACKNOWLEDGEMENTS

I am grateful to the following: Zafar Khan, Diana Morgan and the staff of the Limbless Association for your kind assistance; Zena Al-Ugaily for superb translation; Monica Chakraverty, Richard Johnson and Bartley Shaw at Harper Collins for inviting me to tell Ali's story; Willem Mulder and Susan Warren for your invaluable support in helping me to meet a very tight deadline; zilvester.com for the crisp graphics; Tricia King for commenting so perspicaciously on Iraqi history – any mistakes that remain are of course entirely my own; Susan Quilliam for your insight into why we are primed to focus our attention on innocent victims of war; Mohammed Abd Hamza Al-Sultani, Dr Ahmad Al-Shatti, Dr Ibrahim el-Sayed Ghoneim, Dr Imad Al-Najada, Nafisah Kamal, Dr Sellaiah Sooriakumaran, Nick Hillsdon, Stan East, Fiona Carnegie, Tim Hobbs, Peter Wilson, Andrea Catherwood, Roger Corke, Alexandra Williams, Chris Garwood, Zainab Hashim, Catherine Ecolivet, Mohammed Al-Bader, Stewart Innes and Thomas Edwards for the clarity of your recollections; Mayada Al-Askari for sharing your own disturbing story; Abbie Fielding-Smith for prompt transcription work; Express Newspapers; and of course Ali Ismaeel Abbas, for helping me to understand.

Prologue

Four crumpled photographs spill from the large brown envelope on to a tabletop in South London. They were rescued from the rubble of a burning farmhouse in Baghdad, just before they caught fire. Sadly, no-one could do the same for the people they depict. These are the only images Ali Ismaeel Abbas has to remember his family by.

In one small black and white portrait his winsome mother, Azhar, stares straight out at the camera, her long brown hair tucked under a patterned *hijab*, or religious headscarf. She looks slightly uneasy at being the subject of a photograph and wears just the ghost of a smile. The single surviving picture of Ali's father, Ismaeel, dates from 1983. It shows a tall, rakishly handsome man wearing flip-flops and a brown *dishdashah*, the long-sleeved one-piece garment favoured by men in Middle Eastern countries. He has curly black hair and a black moustache. Looking at the photograph of Ali's brother, Abbas, who was 10 years old when he was killed in his sleep, you can see that he has the same soulful hazel eyes as his older brother.

Finally, there is a picture of Ali himself, posing for a studio photograph with his mother and brother a few years ago. He looks just like any other carefree boy, smiling goofily at a camera. His mother's hand rests gently on his left shoulder.

Two arms hang casually by his sides.

*   *   *

Ali Ismaeel Abbas was born into conflict. When Saddam Hussein invaded the neighbouring State of Kuwait on 2 August 1990, Azhar Ali Dhahir was three months pregnant with her first child. Her baby, a boy named Ali Ismaeel, was born on 9 February 1991, exactly 23 days after the start of Operation Desert Storm. He was just 19 days old when the ceasefire was announced.

Twelve years later, in the early hours of 31 March 2003, a stray missile missed its intended target on the south-eastern fringes of Baghdad, and slugged instead into the heart of a simple farming village where Ali lived in a small concrete house with his family.

In the ensuing fireball Ali lost his mother, who was five months pregnant, his father and his little brother. Thirteen other members of his extended family also died that night: three cousins and their mother, Ali's aunt Kameela; Kameela's sister Madeeha and her husband were also killed, together with their six children and her husband's sister.

Ali also lost his independence. 'Whenever I see Ali, I feel as though he's lost four limbs,' says his legal guardian, Mohammed Abd Hamza Al-Sultani. 'His mother, his father and his two arms.'

PART ONE

Iraq

CHAPTER ONE

'Help me get my Arms Back'

'I remember the night of the bombing each time a plane flies near, I remember the time a plane flew near and started bombing us. We had all gone to bed and we were asleep. We huddled together when we heard the noise of the plane. Suddenly there was a whoosh, the ceiling opened and there was fire and smoke everywhere. It was about midnight when the rocket fell on us. I was in my mother's lap. At first I thought it was a dream: I was under something; then I realized the house had fallen down. Then a lot of strange people came and pulled me out and took me to hospital. I remember hearing screaming. I think it was my aunt asking for a car to take me to hospital. I felt very scared. I kept shouting for my mother, who was five months pregnant. I did not know at the time what had happened to her.

'I remember feeling thirsty. But I was told I couldn't have anything to eat or drink because I had to have an operation. The doctor said, "There is no hope for this boy: he will die." But my 14-year-old cousin, Layth, who had come to the hospital because he was injured, told me not to worry. I was put under anaesthetic. Then there is nothing until I woke up in that hospital and found they

**had cut my arms off. Everything was blurry. I cried when
I realized I didn't have my arms anymore.'**

Ali Ismaeel Abbas, aged 12

On the last day of March 2003 Baghdad awoke to the
heartbreaking lament of the *muezzin*, as its inhabitants were
called again to prayer. The city was shrouded in a thick pall of
black smoke that draped darkly over the slender minarets and
onion-shaped cupolas of the mosques – an attempt by the Iraqi
Republican Guard to hamper US and British air-strikes.

During the previous night the sky had filled with the scream
of low-flying fighter aircraft blasting targets in the south-eastern
suburbs of the city, the thud of bombing, and the retort of anti-
aircraft fire replying furiously from the ground. The BBC
reported that the rumble of explosions – some of the heaviest
bombing since the war began – had been almost continuous,
part of a sustained campaign of round-the-clock coalition air-
strikes that had begun 10 days earlier. They were designed to
break down the resistance of Iraqi troops, loyal to a brutal and
determined dictator, prior to the arrival of US ground troops
in Baghdad. As the barrage of American missiles found new
targets, including a military warehouse in the city's southern
suburbs, the velvet darkness was seared with macabre fireworks
– tracers fired by Iraqi gunners to help them take aim.

Now, in the half-light of early morning, smouldering bomb-
sites of tangled metal, melted glass and shattered concrete were
buildings stopped in time. As the day wore on, people froze mid-
conversation and guardedly eyed the skies, trying to catch sight
of coalition aircraft soaring at supersonic speeds above the
clouds spiralling above the city. Journalists noted that the robed
inhabitants of Baghdad were smoking more, and complaining of
headaches, backaches and a loss of appetite.

In Al-Kindi General Hospital, in central Baghdad, a little boy
of 12 who had recently awoken from the musty confusion of a

general anaesthetic to discover that both his arms had been amputated, was certain he wanted to die. During the night a stray missile had obliterated his home and family.

He was discovered by a Reuter's journalist and photographer a week later close to death, on a filthy bed, in a Baghdad hospital. A rusted metal cage, the shape of a half-barrel, had been placed over his bed to protect his infected wounds. It was covered in a grubby blanket. His charred torso tapered off into two wads of white bandages where his arms should have been. His large, hazel eyes – set in a perfect face, the only part of him left unscarred – were charged with an unsettling intensity. He bit his lip in pain and grief, and began to weep for his lost arms, his lost family, his lost life.

Baghdad's hospitals were full of dead and dying children, but it was immediately clear to the journalists that this poised child with the curly black hair had a singular ability to articulate his despair. 'My father died in the attack, my mother too. My mother was pregnant. What I want is my arms back. I want my hands. Can you help get my arms back? Do you think the doctors can get me another pair of hands? I wanted to be an army officer when I grow up, but not any more. Now I want to be a doctor – but how can I? I don't have hands. What can I do? If I don't get a pair of hands, I will commit suicide,' he said.

Such sentiments are not supposed to be uttered by 12-year-old schoolboys. His disturbing words made a lasting impression on everyone who read them, and his mutely eloquent photograph shocked the world.

CHAPTER TWO

A Happy Boy from a Poor Family

'I used to love my bed: it was a great bed. I slept in that same wooden bed all the time. If they had bought me another bigger bed, I would have refused it. I always slept in that same old bed. Sometimes I would wait up late for my father to come home and he might bring me a treat, like some sweets, to eat.

'Another favourite thing of mine was my father's car. I used to watch it all the time. I was always eyeing that steering wheel. One day my father noticed me looking at it and said, "Ali, would you like to drive?" The first time I tried, the engine just switched off by itself, but soon I was able to drive around the field by myself. I was 10 when I started driving, you know. Once I took the car with my brother, Abbas. We went across to the farm and he kept telling me go this way, go that way. It was so funny. Then, suddenly, we dropped into the mud. It was terrible! I was a bit worried about what my father would say: the car was all muddy.

'Anyway, while we were stuck and wondering what to do, a 17-year-old neighbour came and said, "You're stuck in the mud and you don't know how to drive." I looked at him and I said, "Yes I do and I'm going to get it out." I knew how to drive it and so I got it out by myself. I drove it back to our house and it was all muddy, so we washed it before our father could see it. One day my parents were going to give me a present to celebrate the end of Ramadan, but I said, "I don't want a present – just let me drive!"'

Ali Ismaeel Abbas

The walls were made of concrete breezeblocks, painted blue. There was a roof of corrugated iron, and a smooth concrete floor covered in richly patterned rugs. It wasn't a large or complicated house – just two bedrooms, a kitchen and a bathroom – but this was the only home Ali had ever known. It was built in 1971, 20 years before Ali's birth, by his father, Ismaeel Abbas Hamza, a farm worker and taxi driver who was born in 1953.

Surrounded by farmland spiked with date palms and orange trees, it lay in the heart of the Arab Al-Khrsa – a cluster of eight equally modest concrete farm workers' cottages – and was prone to flooding from the nearby tributary to the mighty Tigris, where Ali liked to fish during the hot summer months.

Ali occupied the smaller of the two bedrooms with his mother, who was born in 1972, his father and younger brother, Abbas. In the other bedroom lived his father's first wife, Layla – referred to fondly as 'Mama Layla' by Ali and his brother – together with Ali's six half-sisters and his half-brother, Hamza. Both bedrooms had doors that led to the simply furnished kitchen. An outside door, painted blue, led to a simple, lean-to bathroom equipped with lavatory, basin and shower.

His family of 12 had few luxuries, but Ismaeel had worked hard to provide a fridge and a mincemeat grinder, a food mixer and a tape recorder, a radio and a television. There was a tap connected to the mains water supply, but no telephone. The electricity supply was sporadic, but sometimes cartoons played upon a small television set in his family's shared bedroom, and Ali loved those.

Ali didn't have many toys, but he did have a tyre attached to a wire that could be coaxed to roll through the dust, and he had a football and a new green bicycle he had recently customized with a can of grey spray paint. When he was seven, his father had bought him a second-hand bike, but when he was eleven he'd received this brand new one: a gift of independence that seemed to exceed the limits of happiness. He spent hours racing through dust or plunging into muddy puddles, depending on the weather, scraping his knees when his tricks failed to come off quite right.

The small farming village of Arab Al-Khrsa is situated down a pot-holed dirt track off Highway 6, the main road south to Basra and Kuwait, 21 kilometres south-east from the centre of Baghdad. The other seven houses were home to many of Ali's uncles, aunties and cousins. It seemed a safe enough place for a child to grow up. A mile across the fields where a few skinny cattle and sheep grazed, grain crops struggled to survive the heat, and where occasional patches of broad beans and tomatoes reached irrigated plumpness, Ali's uncle Mohammed lived with his wife, Shatha, and their five children.

The 160 hectares of farmland around the small suburban town of Za'Faraniya are divided into 8-hectare smallholdings. For many years Ali's father had cultivated one of these plots. Like the other tenant farmers in District 38, Ismaeel was free to build a house on his rented field, and to grow what he liked. In return, he was required to pay his landlord 50 per cent of his income as rent.

Throughout his childhood, Ali was surrounded by attentive females. His half-sisters, aunties and cousins all doted on the gorgeous baby with the joyful chuckle and the huge brown eyes. He also benefited from the love of his two mothers, both of whom had breastfed him when he was a baby. The decision that both women would feed the new baby isn't as surprising as it sounds. This is a traditional arrangement in polygamous house-

8

holds; such intimate sharing of resources helps create a strong and intimate bond between the different strands of a man's family, and it meant that as Ali grew up, he was never short of people to love and cuddle.

Uncle Mohammed had been overjoyed when in 1978 his sister Layla had married their cousin Ismaeel Abbas Hamza (like many working-class marriages in Iraq theirs was arranged), and he became a devoted uncle to each of Ali's sisters. The girls were much loved, but like many men, Ismaeel craved a son.

Under Islamic tradition polygamy is acceptable in Iraq, and a man is able to take up to four wives. The women are expected to live alongside each other, sharing the child-rearing and the homemaking – an arrangement that works with varying degrees of success, depending on the personalities of those involved.

It was Ali's uncle Mohammed who had suggested to Ali's father, Ismaeel, that he should consider taking a second wife in an attempt to have his longed-for heir. 'Because we thought it would be nice to have a boy as well, the family encouraged him to marry again,' says Mohammed, who played matchmaker for a second time when he suggested that Ismaeel should consider marrying Azhar, the gentle and beautiful daughter of another of their cousins, Ali, whom he had watched growing up next door since she was a little girl. There was a bit of gossip about the fact that Mohammed was suggesting his own sister's husband should take a second wife, so the wedding, in 1989, was a fairly quiet, low-key affair.

Ismaeel's first wife, Layla, didn't like what was happening at first, but fortunately the older woman – Layla is seven years older than Ali's mother – took the daughter of her cousin under her wing and they soon became genuinely close. Ismaeel built the second bedroom on to the house after the wedding.

Layla encouraged Azhar's relationship with her daughters, and she was delighted in February 1991 when Azhar gave birth to Ali, amidst much family rejoicing. The family needed some good news: three weeks earlier, during the first Gulf War, part of a stricken American fighter jet had crashed into Mohammed's house. 'The aeroplane fell into the biggest room in my house, damaging my fridge and the sofa suite and breaking the window glass,' recalls Mohammed. Fortunately, no-one was at home at the time. 'Ismaeel and I had taken our families away from Baghdad and had come back to prevent the houses being looted. I was sleeping in Ismaeel's house the night it happened, and found the aeroplane in my house when I returned home the following morning. Ismaeel and my neighbours helped drag it out. Wreckage was strewn over a wide area. We thanked God that no-one was killed. We believe that lightning never strikes in the same place twice, so we immediately went to collect our families and brought them home for the duration of the war.'

When Ali was one year old, both his mothers became pregnant at the same time and, within the space of six weeks, both gave birth to baby boys, who were named Abbas and Hamza. The half-brothers went by the surname Ismaeel Abbas, a combination of their father and paternal grandfather's first names – the traditional construction of names in Middle Eastern countries. 'There was always a special place for Ali because he was the firstborn boy. He was outgoing so he was also very popular,' says Mohammed, who saw him often. 'We could always tell what was going on because my wife had very good eyesight and said she could see across the field between our houses!'

Sometimes Ali went to the market in Baghdad with his father to buy groceries, but the edges of the fields in Za'Faraniya were the real boundaries of his world. He was a happy boy from a poor family, who loved going to school. He worked hard and was always smartly dressed. Shielded and cosseted with all the love his family could give him, for the first few years of his life the small boy was unaware of the troubles besetting his country. As for America and England, they were places he had read about in geography lessons (his favourite subject), but they meant little more to him than curiously shaped maps on a page.

However, in Za'Faraniya the dense urban sprawl of Baghdad gives way not just to farmland, but also to light industry and a number of large warehouse complexes. In December 2002 United Nations weapons inspectors arrived in the town to examine two of these factories: the Modern Chemical Industries Company, which produces industrial alcohol distilled from grain, and the Yafa Juice Company. The investigators suspected that Saddam Hussein had spread his nuclear, chemical and biological weapons plants around the country. It was their conviction that the alcohol- and juice-processing plants they found inside the factories near Ali's home were part of Saddam's 'dual-use' arsenal – equipment that could easily be modified to produce substantial quantities of deadly biological agents.

Ali's hardworking agricultural family can trace their lineage back 1400 years, however they were unaware of their modern-day surroundings. They did not know that the two innocuous-looking Za'Faraniya factories near their farmland had been fingered as probable locations for the manufacture of weapons of mass destruction. Furthermore, they were unaware that the 60-acre Ash Shaykili Warehouse Complex that nestled snugly against the south-eastern contour of Za'Faraniya, had contained some 80 missiles. They were also oblivious to the existence of a suspected missile factory on the outskirts of the town, the Nida State Establishment for Dies and Moulds.

Perhaps most sinister of all from the point of view of the bemused local residents was the uncloaking in early April 2003 of a once heavily guarded nuclear fortress just two kilometres south of Za'Faraniya. High mud bunkers had been engineered with the express intention of hiding the Al-Tuwaythah Nuclear Research Centre from the surrounding villages. This vast steel and marble city had also been examined during the previous autumn for possible evidence of weapons of mass destruction.

None was found. But on 8 April 2003, nine days after the strike on Ali's home, US Marine Corps combat engineers discovered an unknown underground city here, a warren of laboratories, offices and warehouses full of barrels of radioactive material. By the time the American soldiers secured the site in early May, much of the uranium had gone missing. Local people reported that the looters tipped out the deadly substance on to the ground because they wanted these large containers to store food and water. Ali may have lived in the countryside, but his home was far from a pastoral idyll.

CHAPTER THREE
The Flour Went Black

'We were a very simple family. We had only two bedrooms. There were 12 of us and one sister got married, so then we were 11. Our home was very small. Not a tent, just a very simple shack; it certainly wasn't luxurious. We used to laugh a lot in our family. I was very happy.

'I liked playing football with my cousins, neighbours and friends. We played in a small courtyard near our house, close to the river. We would gather there. I had been playing a long time, since I was about nine. I used to love boxing and football. We didn't have many toys, so that's what we did. I had a football and we also had a tyre tied to a wire that we could roll along.

'We used to do as we were told, but we also used to fight, fight, fight, all the time. Our family were always telling us off, but they weren't real troubles. It's just that my brother, Abbas, used to be, well, not grumpy, and not exactly angry … it's just that he gets nervous easily. I'll tell you what it was like. For example, one day when we were playing football, the ball got kicked into another boys' game. They started destroying the ball, so Abbas went up to them very angrily and then I came over to help – and he

fled! And I was left to deal with the consequences. I really
don't know why he always flees.'

Ali Ismaeel Abbas

As Ali was growing up in his small village on the outskirts of
Baghdad, rolling his tyre through the dust and playing football
with his younger brothers, he was unaware that increasing
numbers of children were dying of malnutrition in his country
every year. Since 1990, the year before his birth, infant mortality
rates in Iraq had steadily risen to among the highest in the
world. By 1999 chronic malnutrition affected a quarter of all
children and only 41 per cent of the population had access to
clean water. Low-birth-weight babies had risen from 4 per cent
to around a quarter of all registered births. In 1998 the United
Nations Children's Fund (Unicef) estimated that between 5000
and 6000 Iraqi children were dying every month. A year later
Unicef estimated that, during the eight years from 1991 to 1998,
half a million Iraqi children under five died needless deaths.

Yet in the early days of Saddam Hussein's regime Iraq was a
prosperous country that enjoyed Western standards of living.
Baghdad had elegant shops on fine avenues, beautiful houses set
in elaborate gardens, fine arts, an intelligentsia and a thriving
middle class. In the early 1980s, Iraq – the world's second-
largest producer of oil – boasted one of the highest standards of
living in the Middle East. But on 6 August 1990, four days after
Saddam's army invaded the neighbouring State of Kuwait,
everything began to change. The international community
declared his empire-building unlawful, the UN Security Council
imposed economic sanctions on Iraq, and the country began its
backward slide. All imports, except medical supplies, and all
exports were now prohibited by international law.

The tough trade conditions, described by a spokesman from
the US State Department as 'the toughest, most comprehensive
sanctions in history', were supposed to weaken Saddam's regime

and encourage Iraqi people to revolt against their leader. Revolution was a luxury they could ill afford. The minds of 24 million Iraqis were full of much more important issues: finding the next meal for their families (the average Iraqi family has five children) or sourcing medicine for a sick relative. 'The Iraqi people were told to think of freedom, democracy and changing the regime while they were watching their dearest dying... sanctions left the population increasingly weakened and isolated,' says Haifa Zangana, an Iraqi painter and writer who is the co-founder of Act Together: Women against Sanctions and War on Iraq. In December 1995 she sent an A4 padded envelope from London to her nieces and nephews in Mosul, Iraq's third largest city. It contained one pencil case, three erasers, three sharpeners, six fountain pens, two markers, one glue-stick and two Biros. It was marked 'gift for children'. The envelope was returned, stamped, 'Due to international sanctions against Iraq, we are not able to forward your packet.'

When sanctions first came into force in April 1991, Ali was a nursing baby of just two months old. His uncle remembers that the flour – the nation's staple food – went black overnight. 'Anything to hand was made into flour including date pits, corn cobs and wood shavings,' says Mohammed. 'One day I saw someone selling half-price flour from the back of a truck. The sacks were very heavy – someone discovered they were half-full of cement.'

Basic foodstuffs were soon hard to come by and soared in price. 'A kilogram of sugar used to cost a quarter of a dinar [50 pence] but had gone up to 4000 dinars. The poor-quality flour was soon selling at 10,000 dinars for a sack,' says Mohammed. Fraud was widespread. 'People at the market used syringes to siphon sugar from inside sealed sacks that they then sold at full price.'

When sanctions began, a nation was united by the urge to feed their families by whatever means they could. Ali's mother,

Azhar, cultivated a vegetable patch where she grew onions, garlic and other produce to feed the family. 'Anyone with a garden immediately dug it over to grow vegetables and put animals and chickens to live on them,' says Mayada Al-Askari, scion of an aristocratic Iraqi family, and a former journalist. 'We grew our own food not as a luxury, but for survival. It is difficult for people elsewhere to imagine how bad the situation was.'

Ali's family struggled to cope at first. 'Everyone's reaction was to immediately stockpile all the important foods, such as sugar, rice, oil, flour and soap,' remembers Mohammed. 'But we had no money to buy these things. I had just been discharged from military service and although before sanctions I was a building contractor, I was now on a very small salary. Even if the prices had stayed the same, we couldn't have afforded to buy such large quantities.'

The family may have been poor, but they were lucky to be living on a virtual goldmine: a piece of dust that was suddenly a rich resource. Ali was still a toddler when his uncle and father set to planting every corner of their rented eight-hectare plot with wheat. Their energy paid dividends when they enjoyed an abundant harvest. 'Allah helped us,' says Mohammed, smiling at the memory. 'Our land yielded 32 tonnes of wheat, from which we made a good profit. It was as if He had looked down and challenged the sanctions. We all tried to make it good for the children. We worked hard to keep them healthy,' he says.

Ali's father, Ismaeel, invested his share of the profits from the harvest in a taxi. He worked hard, driving his taxi around the centre of Baghdad, sometimes for 12 hours a day. The following year they planted a second crop, but as they could not afford to condition the soil, the land yielded only a sparse six tonnes. Mohammed started repairing agricultural machinery to make ends meet. 'I worked really hard, but the money I earned covered only food and clothing. We couldn't afford any luxuries at all,' he recalls. Even petrol was hard to come by because of a shortage of the chemicals needed to turn Iraq's oil into usable fuel. 'It was so scarce that you were only allowed to buy what there was on certain days, depending on whether your car registration had an even or odd number in it,' he explains.

Ali may not have had many toys, but there was great fun to be had in inventing games and making up his own. He swam, ran, fed the animals, played football with his friends, and spent hours teasing his beloved half-sisters. He had the richest resource of all: the combined love of his extended family. If his natural mother was unavailable to listen to his stories or sympathize when he fell over, then Layla would offer him her attention and affection instead. He sensed that his father loved both mothers equally. If he was kind to one, he was kind to the other. Ali had noticed that both of them were taken frequently to visit their families.

As Ali was growing up, Iraq experienced a shift from relative affluence to massive poverty. Clean water became a luxury. So did effective waste disposal. Within five years average shop prices of essential commodities stood at 850 times the July 1990 level. Not surprisingly, ordinary Iraqis suffered a severe deterioration in their standard of living, and the middle classes vanished. Their children were starving, their clothes turned to rags and everything began a gradual journey towards disintegration: from smoke-belching buses with broken windows to shops with empty shelves and boarded-up façades. Soon there was illness, suffering, corruption, dilapidation and misery in every corner of the country. One university-educated Iraqi woman wrote in a letter to a British friend, 'We women spend most of our time doing what our grandmothers used to do: we are staying home, sieving flour, baking bread, preparing and storing tomato purée and raising chickens.'

As time went on and the situation worsened, many hungry

families were forced to sell their possessions. When their jewellery and furniture had gone, they began to dismantle their houses. 'People would sell their furniture, then their window frames and then the internal doors,' says Mohammed. 'Finally, when everything that could be sold was sold, they would be forced to sell the land and what remained of the house.' Mohammed says that a wooden door would buy enough food for a family for a week. 'I was able to feed my children well enough, thank God, so we did not have to sell our possessions. But I have neighbours who sold their window frames, doors, beds and clothes to survive. We were lucky to have the taxi and the land.' Many hundreds of desperate parents felt they had no choice but to hand over to the authorities the children they could no longer feed.

Mohammed says that the first five years of sanctions were the hardest. 'After the oil-for-food agreement, things got a bit easier,' he says, referring to the accord Iraq reached with the UN that allowed it to sell $1 billion worth of oil every 90 days, with the money set aside for food and medicine. Every Iraqi citizen was dependent on their ration card, which entitled them to receive the meagre state handouts of cooking oil, soap, sugar, tea and just two kilograms of rice every 10 days. In November 1995, Unicef estimated that the ration card supplied just a third of the calories needed to survive and that doubling this would cost a family of five nearly 100,000 dinars. Yet the average income of 70 per cent of Iraqi families was just 6000 dinars per month.

Mohammed remembers that the quality of flour improved after the oil-for-food agreement, and that there was more of it available, but life was still difficult for many people. 'Not a day went by in 12 years when we didn't wish things were different. You could work hard and make some money, but there were never any guarantees that there would be anything to buy with it,' he says. Part of the problem was that the Iraqi government used the oil-for-food revenue inappropriately. A UK Foreign Office press release of 24 November 2002 details how Iraq had submitted orders for '22,000 tons of chewing gum machines, 12,000 tons of mobile phones, 36,000 dishwashers and over three quarters of a million TVs'.

From the time that Ali was a toddler his mother had had a quiet but focused ambition – she wanted Ismaeel to try to save enough money to buy a small piece of land, as an investment for the children. In 1998, when Ali was seven, and after five years of saving, they had finally managed to save 6000 dinars, the equivalent of one month's income. This formidable achievement was enough to buy a 200-square-metre plot near Za'Faraniya. It was a proud day for Ali's family. They had no money left to build a house on it, but at least this patch of earth was theirs. It is a good thing they bought when they did: when Saddam's regime was toppled in April 2003, 6000 dinars were worth no more than US$3.

When Ali was nine years old, his father Ismaeel became seriously ill with a heart condition and rheumatoid arthritis. Born with a hole in the heart, Ismaeel Abbas had suffered with joint pain for years, but now he was in real trouble: it hurt to move and he was short of breath. In Saddam's Iraq it was virtually impossible to get medicine; he was so eager to lay the blame for infant deaths on the Americans that he held back medicine from the hospitals as a propaganda exercise. He let babies die in Baghdad hospitals for want of basic drugs, and blamed sanctions. 'During the first Gulf War our six-month-old baby, Saif, was ill,' Mohammed recalls. 'But the hospital turned him away because there was no medicine available, and he died.'

Now Ismaeel was ill. He had to come up with a solution so he could continue to support two wives and nine children. 'We had worked together on the farm, planting together, and he had a lot of confidence in me,' says Mohammed. 'He offered to register his car in my name so I could take on his taxi-driving business.' The deal was that Mohammed would lease the taxi from Ismaeel, benefiting both families.

When Mohammed walked across the field each day to collect the car, his first passengers of the day were always two small boys, Ali and his brother Abbas. After he had dropped them off at their large primary school, Mohammed would then head into the centre of Baghdad to tout for business.

Ali had grown into an outgoing, popular and intelligent child who was top of his class at school. As Mohammed began to spend more time with him and his brother, they grew to know each other well. By blood, Ali and Mohammed are first cousins once removed. And to be cousins in closely-bonded Iraqi society, with its long history of intimately entwined extended families, is to be only a shade away from being brother and sister. Therefore, Mohammed has always viewed himself as Ali's uncle, as he is in blood to Ali's half-sisters. 'Ali was a very well-dressed boy. His mother made sure that he and his brother were always nicely turned out in clean clothes. Azhar was very devoted to them and very particular about their food,' says Mohammed. 'Ali was good at sport and always pleasing to the eye. His mother used to make sure that both boys studied hard. Ali was also top of his class at school, a bit more clever than my children. I was hoping for a wonderful future for him. I was anticipating that he could have done anything he wanted with his life.'

Mohammed was also close to Ismaeel, Ali's father. 'Ali's father was eight years older than me, and he had a very strong personality,' Mohammed recalls. 'He was merry and he loved to laugh, but he could be volatile. I saw him get into physical fights if someone wronged him. He would react quickly and he might regret that afterwards, so he would usually go back and apologize, but he was also responsible and caring. He would visit his sisters and was always ready to help when someone was in need. And although I was younger than him, if I offered him advice about something, he would take it. We got along well together and we enjoyed each other's company.'

CHAPTER FOUR

'Never Mention his Name'

'I don't like Saddam Hussein. I don't like him at all. I was frightened of him because if anyone talked about him in not a nice way, then Saddam's men would kill them. Occasionally we talked about him at home. Sometimes I was allowed to stay and listen to the discussion. Other times I'd be asked to leave. But you had to be careful never to mention his name outside the house, and I knew not to talk about him in school. I've known that life is difficult for our family since a very, very long time, since I was about seven or eight. I don't know much about sanctions, but I think they are probably something to do with the war that Saddam made. But my parents took good care of us, you know. We were sort of spoiled, really. Whatever we wanted they would buy it for us, like the bicycle or the fishing rod or the football.'

Ali Ismaeel Abbas

For 12 years the Iraqi people struggled to survive while Saddam relished the propaganda value of sanctions. 'The country had been sucked dry; it was a mess, with wars on every border,' says Jean Sasson, an American author who visited Iraq on a research trip in 1999. 'There was often no electricity, there was certainly no air-conditioning in the hospitals, despite the heat. If you were an ordinary Iraqi and you had food, you were lucky.'

Saddam used food to control people. Only his supporters could buy the meat, vegetables and eggs they craved, the little perks that made life bearable. He paid his army officers well, anxious to ensure that the source of his power and continued survival would want for nothing. Inside the 68 ostentatious palaces he had built – his way of demonstrating that he was still in power – he spoiled his cronies, offering them French fashions, Indian silks and Scandinavian fitted kitchen units. 'There is no question that sanctions empowered his regime and gave him yet more control over the people,' says Haifa Zangana, who was born in Baghdad in 1950, and has lived in London since 1976.

Whenever Ali went to the markets in Baghdad with his father, he saw Saddam everywhere. There were 12-metre-high murals of him on horseback in flowing Arab dress or saluting his adoring masses. There were statues, monuments, paintings and photographs. Saddam could be seen wearing army fatigues, Armani suits, judge's robes and fancy military regalia. He was becoming increasingly vain and paranoid – newspapers were obligated to carry his photograph on every front page – but his personality cult was all smoke and mirrors. In Baghdad gas pipes leaked, sewage spilled on to the streets and crime was widespread. Patrick Cockburn, co-author of *Out of the Ashes*, describes watching Saddam reviewing a parade of supposedly elite troops in Baghdad a few years ago. 'From a distance they all looked very impressive in their white gloves. It was only when I got closer that I realized the Iraqi army was as short of gloves as it was of everything else; the men were wearing white sports socks on their hands.'

The Iraqi people are proud and resourceful, but there was no guarantee that even those who had survived the sanctions would live to tell the tale. Saddam had managed to instil fear in the souls of his countrymen with his regime's total disregard for human rights and dignity. His regime was known for killing the innocent without trial. In the 1980s he used chemical weapons against the Kurdish people of Iraq, who were seeking self-government. He ruthlessly oppressed his opponents, but also sought control over the heart and mind of every ordinary citizen. The only way he could stay in power was to terrorize Iraq's population into cowed submission.

In addition to the Mukhabarat, the notorious Iraqi Intelligence Service, the increasingly deranged dictator began to use the party members put in charge of distributing the monthly food rations as an instrument of state control. Gradually these informers became a terrifying force controlling Iraqis' daily lives. 'If they want anything from anyone, they don't give you your rations. So to maintain your family's life you have to do what they want,' explains a former Iraqi schoolteacher. 'We depend upon the family system and the tribe. In our culture your family's life is more important than your own. So you have to do what they want.'

Ali had never known an Iraq that wasn't suffering under sanctions or the devious machinations of Saddam Hussein, but for the first few years of his life he was kept in blissful ignorance about the brutality of Saddam's regime. Before the age of five or six, Iraqi children tended to be shielded from their family's political conversations. Everyone had heard rumours of parents, after their children had guilelessly repeated their words at kindergarten, being snatched by Saddam's security services. The horrific excess of Saddam's sadism indirectly touched Ali's life when the brother of Mohammed's sister's husband was executed without trial in 2000. 'He was 22 years old and had only been married for seven days,' recalls Mohammed. 'He had just graduated from engineering college when he was accused of having some religious papers. He denied the charge, so the commander gave the order to rape his young bride and his sister. So immediately, of course, he spoke up and pretended to have those papers. He was then taken to the headquarters of the secret police, where he was searched. When no religious papers were found, he was paraded in a large open area. Saddam's sons used prisoners like him to hone their shooting skills. After he was executed, his body was given back to the family.'

Saddam's psychopathic son and heir-apparent Uday was notorious for handpicking rape victims from educational colleges or upmarket hairdressers. 'Ali's sisters were safe enough: he wouldn't have come to somewhere like Za'Faraniya,' explains Mohammed. Nevertheless, when the six girls went out, they were always accompanied.

To understand how the modern nation of Iraq had become the horrific playground of a brutal dictator and his psychopathic henchmen, it is necessary to turn the clock back to the time of the Ancient Greeks.

For thousands of years the modern nation of Iraq was part of Mesopotamia, which means 'land between two rivers', an ancient fertile land to the east of the Arabian desert, named by the Ancient Greeks and irrigated by the mighty Tigris and Euphrates. With its rich resources and prime geographical location between the Persian Gulf and the Mediterranean, this lush, cultivated paradise has had a turbulent history, conquering and being conquered by avaricious foreign powers. In the seventh century the Arabs brought the Arabic language, the new Islamic religion and founded the fabulous and exotic city of Baghdad, a jewel of the Near East. The Mongols took over in the thirteenth century and did a thorough job trashing the region before the Ottoman Turks arrived during the sixteenth century and ruled until the First World War, when they sided with the Germans. The British helped the oppressed Arab tribes strike back against the Turks, a successful revolt turned into a twentieth-century legend by David Lean's 1962 multi-Oscar-winning epic, *Lawrence of Arabia*.

At the end of the First World War the Arabs were surprised

to discover that the triumphant Europeans now believed themselves the rightful owners of every resource in the region. The British and the French duly carved up Mesopotamia: the French got Syria, and the British got Iraq. 'They got away with it because Arab nationalism was not yet strong enough to challenge them,' writes historian Margaret Macmillan in *Peacemakers*. The British were keen to enhance their trade routes to India, then under imperial rule. They also had their eye on oil: Iraq has the world's second largest reserves after neighbouring Saudi Arabia.

However, rather than turning his chunk of Mesopotamia into a British colony, as would have happened in the past, the British prime minister Lloyd George declared instead it was to become a new Arab nation state to be called Iraq. 'He was intoxicated by the possibilities [of] loyal and obedient Arab states ... protection for British oil supplies from Persia and the possibility of new sources under direct British control,' writes Macmillan.

In 1921 the British enthroned an Arab king and the country was prepared for independence with its first national government. The ancient and neglected city of Baghdad had regained its dignity. In 1932, two years before Iraq began exporting oil, Britain's authority over Iraq was terminated, and the country became a new, self-governing nation state. Tribal and religious tensions that had been simmering for generations began to boil. For the next 40 years the country rocked from one bloody crisis to another, scarred by a series of military coups and minority uprisings as different factions competed for power.

In 1958 the British-appointed Iraqi royal family were massacred and replaced with the first of a series of military dictators who ruled by the sword. Against this feverish backdrop the Ba'ath Party, a pro-Arab socialist group that came to power in 1968, began to gain influence. Thirty-one-year-old Saddam Hussein won a leading government position, soon followed by the post of vice-president. All the time, he was building a power base in the security services. He may have been the number two, but he was the real power in Iraq, and from 1968 to 1979 was part of a regime that brought improvements in education, health and infrastructure. New schools, roads, public housing and hospitals were built. Saddam believed in primary education for all, schooling for girls and a secular curriculum. The country even earned a Unesco prize for eradicating illiteracy – although those who had refused to attend his reading programme were jailed. Within a few years women could enter any profession they chose. Soon the standard of living in Iraq was equivalent to that in the UK.

'While we still knew him as Mr Deputy we Iraqis were lulled into tranquillity by Saddam's charismatic personality. We believed in his greatness, in the idea of Iraqi self-rule,' says Mayada Al-Askari, a former Iraqi journalist. For only with hindsight did it become clear that all these improvements were part of a twisted master plan, a cynical trust- and confidence-building exercise designed to win hearts and minds that would gain him the uncritical support for which he hungered, and allow him to start crushing other nations. In his book *The Theatre of Politics*, the political historian Ferdinand Mount has analysed why some government regimes last longer than others. He calls the long-lasting ones 'survivor regimes'. The first need of survivor regimes, he argues, is 'to communicate a sense of confidence and to establish stability'.

Once achieved, stability didn't last long. In July 1979 Saddam shunted the ailing president aside and presided over a macabre ceremony in which 66 of his former colleagues in the Ba'ath Party were executed by firing squad. His ambition then turned to conquest. Within months he had plunged his country into the first of a series of brutal conflicts. The invasion of Iran in September 1980 turned into an eight-year war that left 1.5 million dead. During the war ordinary Iraqis woke up to the fact that this unstable dictator who was happy to gas entire Kurdish villages and attack Iran's civilian population, was likely to destroy their own country too.

It was a conclusion reinforced when their power-crazed dictator invaded their tiny neighbour, Kuwait, in August 1990, less than two years after the Iran–Iraq ceasefire. Saddam accused Kuwait of flooding world oil markets and threatening Iraq's attempts to boost its war-torn economy. The United Nations established international trade sanctions against Iraq, but Hussein refused to withdraw his troops. Five months after it started, the occupation of Kuwait was brought to a speedy conclusion in just six weeks by Operation Desert Storm.

The parents of baby Ali, who was 19 days old when the ceasefire was announced, and millions more Iraqis like them, braced themselves for the Allied forces to storm Baghdad and apprehend Saddam. But in place of British and American soldiers came instead the crippling trade sanctions that began to wear everyone down. The sanctions made it difficult for Iraq to feed its population and rebuild itself, but Saddam repeatedly violated terms of the ceasefire, causing continued suffering for ordinary Iraqis. Frequent attempts were made to oust Saddam internally, but none was successful and the consequences of standing up to him became increasingly bloody.

Even innocent Iraqis now found themselves under suspicion as Saddam's security apparatus – the Mukhabarat – grew in stature. Everyone already knew that to criticize President Saddam led to an automatic sentence of tongue removal before death. Now their country had become a police state where ordinary people could be arrested without trial and be accused of crimes such as 'staring' or 'having the wrong papers' before being tortured into submission. No-one was immune.

On 19 July 1999 44-year-old Mayada Al-Askari was arrested by Saddam's secret police and thrown into Baladiyat, the headquarters of Saddam's secret police, which also served as a prison complex. She was accused of printing anti-government propaganda – a crime of which she was innocent. During one interrogation she was held in a room where hooks dangled from the ceiling, and where she saw a table piled high with metal instruments and electrical cables.

The mother of two can recall, in distressing detail, the moment one week later when the electrodes were attached to her quivering body in an attempt to force a 'confession'. 'The big toe on my right foot was squeezed in a clamp. A rough hand pulled back my hair and a second clamp squeezed my right earlobe. Heavy equipment was pulled across the floor,' she recalls, shifting uncomfortably in her seat at the disquieting memory. She says she could hear someone screaming, realized it was herself, and passed out with the pain. Just like the 17 other innocent women with whom she shared a fetid, blood-smeared cell, she had not received a trial. They all faced the same treatment: torture and the threat of execution if they did not confess to their alleged 'crimes'. One woman had been arrested simply because she complained that her rubbish had not been collected.

However, 14 years earlier, Mayada had found herself singled out for a quite different form of attention. Upon the death in 1965 of her celebrated grandfather Sati Al-Husri, revered in the Arab world as the architect of Arab nationalism, Saddam transferred his respect on to this man's family. As a student in Cairo, Hussein had venerated the scholar.

Mayada, a writer of non-political stories for an Iraqi newspaper, was often summoned to one of Saddam's lavishly decorated palaces, where he showered her with praise and awarded her cash 'prizes'. When she was first invited, buffet tables groaned under the weight of beluga caviar and exotic fruit. 'Saddam smiled broadly and told me I was a fitting granddaughter for Sati Al-Husri. He summoned a photographer, and when I left he kissed me on my forehead.' An aide then handed her an envelope containing £6000 and two leather boxes containing watches made of diamonds, silver and gold, that were emblazoned with the dictator's image. On another occasion he gave her two pieces of land in gratitude for a report she had written about extrasensory perception. Mayada met Saddam Hussein six times between 1979 and 1986, and observed at first hand the onset of his mental disintegration as he became more tyrannical with each passing year. She says that she still struggles with the knowledge that the once charming young head of state had developed into the twisted architect of such brutality.

'He was intense, caring and interested in the details of people's lives. I was beguiled by him on those early occasions when we met. I'll admit I was naive,' she says. 'Dictators are always charming.' As the years passed, she was still invited to these private meetings. 'I had no illusions by then, but you could not think about refusing an invitation: I had to protect my family,' she says.

For many years family connections kept Mayada safe, but in 1999 she was arrested, one of 10 print shop owners to be routinely rounded up and tortured after anti-Saddam leaflets were published. Released after three weeks in prison, she fled the country. She is distraught that she has so far not been able to locate a single woman with whom she was imprisoned. When Iraq was liberated in April 2003, many prisoners – human evidence – were executed by the fleeing guards.

Iraq's prisons stand as the most vivid testimony to what life under Saddam was like for many millions. After the Gulf War, a human ear was found nailed to the wall in one prison. Torture chambers held the bodies of recently strangled women and children. His was a culture of violence. People were shown on Iraqi television having their hands amputated for minor misdemeanours. Saddam showed no compunction about using chemical weapons, or about murdering women and children. Dissidents claimed he was personally involved in torturing political prisoners, on one occasion tipping a man into a bath of acid. And his sons inherited his callous gene: the rapist Uday controlled the only Olympic Committee headquarters in the world with its own torture chamber. It was bombed on 1 April in a strike designed to hit Uday – two days after Ali's home was destroyed.

Every member of Ali's immediate family, surviving through a mixture of nous and luck, avoided being captured, tortured or killed by Saddam's merciless government. 'We used to be very careful,' explains Mohammed. 'We just tried to keep our heads down.' The family even stopped attending religious events when they heard that seven hundred people had been thrown into prison for visiting a religious shrine. 'We knew that everyone was vulnerable, not just Shiites like ourselves. His brutality was indiscriminate. Everyone knew that Saddam had had both his sons-in-law killed.' Hussein and Saddam Kamil defected in 1995 and returned to Iraq from Jordan after the Iraqi government announced amnesties for them. They were executed on their return in February 1996.

Iraq was now a dark, forbidding place where everyone was living in poverty and where there was never enough to eat. And so, as the coalition forces began pounding Baghdad – after Saddam Hussein refused to cooperate with the United Nations weapons inspection programme, a course of action that could have led to a suspension of sanctions – Ali's family welcomed their arrival with fatalistic resignation. They were, after all, Shiite Muslims, in a country in which minority Sunni Muslims had always been in control. Perhaps those planes and bombs would bring liberation at last.

CHAPTER FIVE

'We Saw a Missile Fall'

'When the bombs were falling, sometimes I'd get excited like my father. Sometimes we children were really frightened by them. Sometimes we weren't. But if there was an explosion nearby, we used to get really scared. Everyone, that is, apart from my sister Shala'a. She didn't get scared. When the bombing was happening, she always joked and laughed and said, "Oh, I'll go outside and catch a missile." Then there would be a really loud noise, an explosion, and we would all cover our ears. But we never thought that a bomb or missile would fall on us. One day we saw an aircraft being chased through the sky with anti-aircraft fire. Me and my friends were watching that, but we got a bit afraid that one of the missiles might fall on us, so we went and hid in a stream. That stream is usually where the sheep drink. Then we saw a missile fall on some houses about two kilometres away from where we were hiding, and we were scared then.'

Ali Ismaeel Abbas

When the coalition bombardment of Iraq began on 20 March 2003, it was a disturbing reminder for Ali's family of the events of the first Gulf War when a stricken American fighter plane had partially demolished Mohammed's house. Ali had been just a baby during the last bombing campaign. Now he was fully conscious of what was going on. Sometimes he was excited, like his father, by the noise of aeroplanes dropping bombs and by the retort of anti-aircraft fire. At other times, when the bombing felt too close for comfort, he was terrified.

Za'Faraniyah had been subjected to air-strikes during the previous conflict, so Mohammed and Ismaeel decided to evacuate their families to Jbela, a town in Babylon province, 100 kilometres south of Baghdad, where Ismaeel's brother and Mohammed's uncle lived. 'We had very bad memories from 12 years earlier of the horror of the plane falling, so we decided to take the family away from the city immediately,' explains Mohammed. As before, Ismaeel and Mohammed returned to keep the houses safe from looters. Layla and one of Ali's sisters decided to stay as well. Each day Ismaeel drove to Jbela to visit his family.

But during the next few days the province of Babylon also came under fire as US-led ground troops began to advance north towards Baghdad. Ali and his family had unwittingly moved into the front line. On 29 March Mohammed and Ismaeel decided to bring their families home again the following day. 'Nowhere was now safe, but at least this way we could all be together,' Mohammed explains with a shrug of regret. It was to prove to be a tragic decision.

The night before the men left Baghdad to collect their families, fighter jets screamed over their southern suburb and the ground trembled as missiles bombarded their targets 16 kilometres away. With US troops now less than 80 kilometres south of the capital, the coalition air-strikes on Baghdad were intensifying in a bid to weaken the resistance from the Iraqi Republican Guard who were digging in to defend the city.

Mohammed says he will never forget Ismaeel's almost manic excitement at this aerial display, and all it symbolized. 'He rushed outside to watch. My sister Layla was shouting to him to come back inside, to be careful, but Ismaeel ignored her pleas. I remember Ismaeel shouting, "I want to enjoy this, I don't want to forget this. I want to see the American planes do this and then, when they kill Saddam, I am going to invite them for a nice lamb feast, and I'm going to barbecue it like the cowboys do." That's what he said.'

The next day, 30 March, Mohammed and Ismaeel collected their families from Jbela. They arrived back in Za'Faraniya at 6 p.m. and gathered by the river to share their stories of the past eight days. They were very happy to be reunited again. Some people then went home, but a few of them, including Mohammed and Ismaeel, picked broad beans and radishes together. As dusk fell, Mohammed said goodnight to Ali's family, and returned across the fields in preparation for another night of disturbed sleep.

'When the air-raid started, I told the women and children to go downstairs while I went upstairs. The bombs seemed much closer this time. I heard my children crying out, so I went downstairs to calm them. Then at about midnight the house was rocked by several incredibly loud, deep explosions.'

Terrified by their apparent proximity, Mohammed ran up and out on to the roof of his house to see where the bombs had fallen. He could see burning houses in the small hamlet of Arab Al-Khrsa, where Ali's family lived, but the smoke made it impossible to pick out details.

'I ran downstairs shouting for my nephew and we started running across the field. Every time the Iraqi resistance retaliated with anti-aircraft fire the sky would fill with light and we had to throw ourselves down in the field.'

In the pauses between firing, Mohammed and his nephew sprang to their feet and ran as fast as they could towards the burning hamlet.

'When we got there, we realized that four houses had been hit. There was a mass of burning rubble with a few walls still standing, and I saw a huge crater that had been the centre of the impact. It was very disorientating, nothing looked as it had before. It was all damaged and burned, but then I recognized one particular wall because it was painted blue. I knew that it was Ali's house. And there was still fire in it ...'

Disorientated by grief and fear, Mohammed stepped into what remained of the house. 'I lost all sense for a while. Time seemed to be passing and I didn't know what to do, where to start.' Then he heard a voice. 'I got Ali out, but I couldn't help the others,' said a distraught man. Mohammed peered through the smoke; Ali's neighbour, Kareem Jassim Ahmed, was lying in the rubble of Ali's house. 'Be careful. I can't move: I was barefoot and I got electrocuted when I came back inside because the floor was wet,' cried Kareem.

Mohammed was wearing his rubber farm boots. He scrambled through the partially demolished house, desperate to find another living soul. Lying on a bed under fallen masonry he saw a sight he says he will never forget: a charred man, his arms frozen in front of his face as if his last moment had been spent trying to hold up the collapsing roof. It was Ismaeel. Lying next to him were two smaller bodies, Ali's mother and younger brother, also charred black and horribly mutilated. 'Three of them, Ali's family. It was a terrible sight,' he says. 'These images will live in front of my eyes forever.'

He climbed through the rubble to the other bedroom where his nieces and his sister slept. 'I saw the face of the youngest girl and she was staring at me in shock, unable to speak. Once we'd got her outside we started digging into the fallen ceiling with our hands to try and find survivors.' At that moment the civil defence guard arrived and the beams from their flashlights lit up the smouldering ruins of the house as their officer shouted, 'Who do you think is alive? Who sleeps in this room?'

'I told them, six girls and a boy, and their mother.' Assisted by the guards, the digging continued. Suddenly they found Ali's half-sisters and their brother, Hamza, lying in an air pocket, but there was no sign of Layla. 'We're going to dig again,' said the officer. With bleeding hands, Mohammed continued to scrabble in the broken masonry, searching frantically for his sister, Ali's stepmother.

'Hey, somebody's grabbing my foot,' shouted one of the civil defence officers. He reached down and Layla was pulled from the rubble, covered with bloody cuts, but at least she was alive. Others were not so fortunate. Four homes were destroyed by the same bomb that killed Ali's family. In one of them eight members of his extended family were killed.

As the burned and broken bodies were retrieved from the burning rubble, they were placed in a row on the ground outside what had been, just the day before, a happy family house. A place where two boys had played together and looked forward to the birth of a new brother or sister in the summer.

Ali's mother and father had survived the Iran–Iraq War. They had survived the Gulf War. They had survived the sanctions. They had survived Saddam. They had almost had a future, but they were killed by a bomb that was supposed to have brought them freedom and the chance for a new life. 'We'd been waiting for this moment of liberation and when it came it tore us apart,' says Mohammed. 'People were killed. Our homes were blown away. It was very expensive in terms of what it cost our family.'

Ali had been rushed to hospital with terrible injuries in a neighbour's car, but Mohammed's first duty was to the dead. He stayed with the remains until sunrise when the bodies were taken to a hospital morgue by the civil defence officers. He was told to come to Al-Kindi General Hospital on Palestine Street, central Baghdad, later that day to collect them for burial.

The staff at the hospital morgue took photographs of what

remained of Ali's family when they arrived. Looking at these pictures, it is difficult to identify human beings amidst the charred remains, clumps of straw, and scraps of red and green floral fabric.

CHAPTER SIX

'It's a Hopeless Case, Hopeless'

'My father is very kind. His friends love him because he's very helpful. He did so much for me, and worked hard so we could have things. Just before the accident happened, my father saw a wounded Iraqi soldier by the side of the road and took him to hospital.

'Sometimes he would sing at home, classical songs of Iraq. I like the way he sings, but my mother used to like to watch programmes on television. When he's singing, she tells him to shut up. Then, only when the programme is over, will he stop! They were always joking and teasing each other. He used to love her a lot.'

Ali Ismaeel Abbas

Weapons don't always work. Although the lion's share of the bombing in Iraq was carried out by missiles guided by satellite, the American military estimates that 7 to 10 per cent don't hit their targets. A fin breaks off. A computer component malfunctions. These are mechanical devices and some will always fail. When this happens, military targets are left unscathed and the bombs fall instead on to some unintended location. Dropped from a plane and hurtling towards its target at 480 kilometres per hour, a four-metre steel-encased missile uses small gears in its fins to steer towards its target, while using satellite data received by a small antenna and fed into an onboard computer. Just before impact a fusing device triggers a chemical reaction, causing the 36-centimetre-wide weapon to swell to twice its size. As the bomb hits the target, the steel casing shatters and spews out hundreds of pounds of white-hot fragments travelling at close to the speed of sound. It gouges a five-metre-wide crater as it displaces thousands of pounds of rock and earth, and generates a shock wave that can knock down walls.

It is all too easy to imagine how effortless it was for that lethal blast to flatten Ali's simple home, as his parents and brother were roasted alive in the ensuing fireball.

People who saw the devastation of Ali's home said it seemed extraordinary that anyone could have survived. 'All that remains from the strike by the stray missile is a pile of rubble and charred wood,' reported the *Daily Mirror*'s Stephen Martin from Arab Al-Khrsa nearly two weeks later. 'Scattered about outside are a few pairs of sandals, bits of bedding and a melted hairdryer.' He saw the carcasses of 30 cattle killed in the explosion and the twisted remains of Ismaeel's pride and joy, the 15-year-old silver Toyota he had just finished overhauling.

Ali was asleep when his world stopped a little before midnight on the night of 30 March 2003, on the ninth day of the war. Mercifully, his memory of that terrible experience is eroding with the passage of time and in the retelling. He now says he was alone in his bed, but he used to believe he was curled up against his mother's lap, sharing a bed with her.

Other dreadful details do not vary. 'Suddenly there was a whoosh, the ceiling opened and there was fire everywhere,' he says, fidgeting in his seat and scuffing his trainers on the ground beneath as he speaks in a confident voice. As his bed sheets burned, he recalls screaming or shouting. He says he was lifted up into the air or dragged out sideways across the floor. He says it was difficult to know then whether he was awake or asleep. But he is certain that he called for his mother over and over again.

Ali's arms were incinerated. His torso and back were terribly badly burned. Yet somehow his face and head escaped injury. It still seems like a miracle. If indeed he was in bed with his mother, perhaps she instinctively reached to protect his head with her body, in what became a final embrace for them both.

Ali may have been the only member of his immediate family to survive the missile strike, but he was in a critical condition. Placed on the back seat of a neighbour's car, he was driven immediately to the local hospital. Doctors there took one look at his terrible wounds and said they were unable to deal with his horrific injuries. They told the neighbour to take him to one of Baghdad's principal hospitals, a half-hour drive away.

After a few kilometres, the car was forced to stop at a roadblock at the southern approach to the city. The Iraqi soldier gruffly interrogated the driver, 'Where are you going? Where are you headed?' Catching sight of a moaning bundle of rags in the back seat, crying for its mother, he asked 'Who is this?' and shone his torch into Ali's eyes. The light was dazzling. Instinctively, Ali moved to cover his face, but found his arms did not seem to be responding. He realized that he couldn't feel his fingers move either. He felt frightened as he heard the soldier mutter gravely, 'It's a hopeless case, hopeless.'

The hospital to which the boy was being taken was no sanctuary. The Al-Kindi General Hospital was named after a famous Iraqi scholar and philosopher from the eighth century AD. Before the conflict, it was one of Iraq's teaching hospitals, with 250 beds, 12 operating theatres and more than 60 senior doctors skilled in trauma surgery, as well as specialities including neurology, and ear, nose and throat; but at the start of the bombing campaign it was one of five hospitals designated as a first-line treatment centre for civilian casualties. All non-essential departments had been closed down and the windows shrouded with piles of sandbags.

Now, on the tenth day of the war, conditions were deteriorating rapidly. Flies clustered around open wounds and blood caked the sheets. Wards were running out of clean water, the electricity supply was intermittent, and there was a shortage of equipment to treat burns and shrapnel wounds. Lengths of steel and moulding clay substituted for fracture-fixing frames, and most patients facing emergency surgery could be given no more than 800 milligrams of Ibuprofen, equivalent to four Nurofen tablets. The doctors felt overwhelmed by the sharp rise in casualties since US ground troops began to close in on Baghdad and the coalition aerial assault intensified. During fierce bombardment up to 100 casualties an hour were arriving.

Bleeding bodies, many of them moaning in untreatable pain on improvised stretchers made from blankets and bed sheets, stretched down the corridors in all directions. Painkilling drugs, already in short supply before the bombing started, were now non-existent. Ambulances arrived constantly, ferrying new victims, as the streets outside boiled with terror and confusion. Other casualties limped in on foot, shocked, bleeding and disorientated.

Many medical staff were unable to cross the city to work because of the bombing. Those who could work stayed in shelters at the hospital: it was far too dangerous to travel home. They were assisted by doctors from other Baghdad hospitals as well as those from the charity Médecins sans Frontières. Most staff worked punishing 24-hour shifts.

Even experienced medics who had treated victims of the 1980–88 Iran–Iraq War and the 1991 Gulf War were shocked at the scale and extent of the injuries they were being confronted with, hour after hour. The hospital's assistant director, Dr

Osama Saleh Al-Duleimi, told journalists, 'I've been a doctor for 25 years, and this is the worst I've seen in the number of casualties and fatal wounds.' In this war many of the targets lay close to civilian neighbourhoods.

There were shortages of anaesthetic, painkillers and staff. Most dangerously, the hospital, which felt more like a military facility on the front line than a civilian hospital, was no longer sterile. It was a dangerous and frightening destination, and certainly no place for a little boy with horrific third-degree burns, in need of life-saving surgery.

When Dr Saleh, an experienced orthopaedic surgeon, first saw Ali's injuries, he wanted to weep. He had trained in Cuba in the branch of medicine dealing with the correction of deformities of bones or muscles, but what could he do for this 12-year-old boy, a child who was the same age as his daughter? He knew that Ali, being deeply burned, could feel only moderate pain due to the damage to his nerves; but he also knew that the chances of his surviving more than a few weeks were slender at most. 'These burned people have complications after three or four days. In the first week they usually get septicaemia,' he said. He expected Ali to be dead within three weeks.

Bacteria had already begun to multiply inside the burns that covered 35 per cent of the boy's body. The fire had consumed muscle and fat on his torso to a depth of almost 2.5 centimetres in places, but this was a blessing of sorts – the most severe burns had incinerated his nerve endings and cauterized the flow of blood. However, without urgent medical intervention his traumatized body would soon yield to catastrophic organ failure as his blood was slowly poisoned by the build-up of toxins.

'I remember hearing one of the medical staff saying, "There is no point: this kid is going to die. Let's move on to someone we can save,"' says Ali. But evidently a decision was taken to do two basic amputations. As the doctors examined him, Ali remembers begging for water. 'I was told I couldn't have anything to eat or drink because I had to have an operation,' he recalls.

Just before surgery, surgeons took photographs of Ali's naked, untreated body. These are profoundly upsetting images and have never been published in the mainstream media. Looking at them, it is clear why. They are just too shocking. The truth is that if Ali had been found by journalists before surgery – and the tidy application of cream and bandages – his image would have been judged too upsetting for publication. In the colour snaps the boy is lying naked in the emergency operating theatre, his face covered by a white anaesthesia mask. An oval of charred flesh dominates his torso, reaching from his shoulder to his hip. It looks as if an inky puddle of oil has pooled there. Around its perimeter is a fringe of livid red tissue, the painful second-degree burns. And then there is what remains of his arms.

The first journalist to see these photographs and to describe the devastation of Ali's burned limbs in print was the experienced American foreign correspondent and essayist Jon Lee Anderson, writing in *The New Yorker*. On Monday 7 April his weekly 'Letter from Baghdad' was subtitled 'War Wounds'. 'At about the biceps, the flesh of both arms became charred, black grotesqueries. One of his hands was a twisted, melted claw. His other arm had apparently been burned off at the elbow, and two long bones were sticking out of it. It looked like something that might be found in a barbeque pit.'

Consent to amputate needed to be obtained from Ali's next of kin. It was given by Ali's maternal uncle, Hamza. 'The doctor told him Ali's arms had to be amputated, but Hamza begged him to save his arms,' says Mohammed. 'He realized that life would be difficult for him and he was desperate to see if there was an alternative.' There was not. The doctor was insistent: without the surgery Ali would die.

A few days earlier there had not been enough electricity to

power the operating theatres, but fortunately a sixth reserve generator had just been installed in the operating theatre by Red Cross workers, allowing surgery to continue. The charity had also provided a number of fresh surgical sets, dressings and instruments, a limited stock of anaesthetics, and piles of clean blankets. They had also delivered thousands of bags of clean water to Al-Kindi, allowing staff to sterilize their surgical instruments.

After the operation, Ali was taken down a bare corridor where a portrait of Saddam Hussein hung on the wall, and into a small room lit by a patch of sunlight from a tiny window. Still unconscious, he was settled on the bed and a curved metal cage painted green was pulled into position above his torso and covered in a coarse brown blanket.

The tender, multicoloured flesh on Ali's chest and tummy had now been smeared with thick white antiseptic cream in lieu of skin. This was the only method the doctors had of protecting his exposed flesh from bacterial invasion. They knew it was just a temporary solution. The boy was in need of sophisticated skin-graft surgery from a specialized burns unit. In Baghdad such treatment was now unthinkable. It was unlikely he would survive long enough to get the treatment he needed.

Dr April Hurley of Santa Rosa, California, spent several weeks in Iraq with the humanitarian group Voices in the Wilderness, visiting hospitals during the bombing campaign. She was at Al-Kindi when Ali arrived and saw him just after his arms were amputated.

'Ali had incredible third-degree burns on his torso,' she says. 'Most of his chest and abdomen was third-degree burned. That whole area of skin would have to be removed and replaced with other skin. Any doctor could tell that he faced the risk of infection, which is difficult to control with antibiotics, even in a specialized sterile burns unit. He faced the terrible pain to come of having his dressings removed and replaced, as well as future surgery and months of rehab, not to mention the emotional trauma he would have to deal with once he was told all his family had been killed.'

More immediately, Dr Hurley was concerned about the quality of the amputations that had been carried out in such difficult circumstances. 'I didn't think they were safe,' she explains. 'I was worried those sites were going to break down. One shoulder had a length of bone retained and covered over with skin and muscle. As he grows, that bone will have to be cut back, or else it will extend and threaten the closure.' She took copies of the pre-surgery photographs of Ali and e-mailed them home to America, but was unable to get them broadcast or published.

At 11 a.m. on 31 March Mohammed travelled to the hospital with nine members of the extended family, including two of Ismaeel's brothers, in a car and a small bus owned by Ali's uncle Hamza. They had come, as requested, to collect the corpses of his dead family; but first of all they went to visit Ali. 'He had just come out of surgery and was still sedated. He didn't know I was there,' recalls Mohammed. 'His arms had been removed and they were lying next to him on the bed, wrapped up in some cloth. Before the accident, Ali was fat, cheerful, beautiful and full of life. Now I thought it would be better if he died. I couldn't see a future for him.'

The amputated arms were placed in a cardboard box so that Mohammed could take them away. Ali's maternal grandfather, Ali, stayed by the boy's bedside. His stepmother, Layla, three of his half-sisters, his uncle, a cousin and five more relatives had also been brought to the hospital a few hours after Ali with fractures, cuts and other minor injuries.

Mohammed then steeled himself to go to the morgue, a small building at the rear of the hospital. The concrete pathway was spattered with blood. Several hypodermic needles lay on the ground. Bloody wheeled stretchers were parked outside. Inside lay the bodies of Ali's mother, father and brother. They had been wrapped up in bandages, as had those of his other 13 family members. Their faces remained uncovered. It was a truly distressing sight. So were the mechanics of taking them for burial. 'We had to hire a pickup truck. We lined it with a large plastic sheet and lay seven of the bodies on this. There wasn't enough room for everyone, so we also hired another bus for the other nine,' says Mohammed.

Sometime during the afternoon of 31 March Ali woke up and saw bandages where his arms should have been. He was engulfed with despair. 'Everything was blurry when I woke up. I cried when I realized I didn't have my arms,' he says. All his hopes for the future now seemed impossible. How could he be a soldier if he didn't have arms? Perhaps these doctors could fix his body, give him new skin, and maybe they knew a way for him to get his arms back?

CHAPTER SEVEN

'We Summoned All the Men'

'My mother was a quiet person. She used to cook nice meals and she used to love us a lot. She used to joke with us all the time, and give us lots of cuddles. I love babies and I asked her if she could give me and Abbas another baby to play with. When she said we were going to have another baby, I was so happy. I love them so much. I want to have children of my own. I've got a baby half-sister of seven called Hadeel. I love her a lot. Sometimes I would tease her. Unfortunately, sometimes she would cry when I pinched and cuddled her. She used to spend all her money buying sweets. Then, when I had money, she asked me why I hadn't bought her any balloons!'

Ali Ismaeel Abbas

A funeral is supposed to be a healing ritual of reflective farewell. But for Ali's family such cathartic convention was an unobtainable luxury. Instead, the only means by which the surviving family could honour their dead was to offer them the dignity of a simple grave, dug with their own hands, and hastily covered over before more bombs began to fall.

Islamic funerals are generally quite a hands-off concern, as they are for Christians. The funeral director, or *deffan*, organizes everything, arranging for a body to be taken to the *mghasel*, or undertaker, who prepares it for burial by ritually washing the body, sealing all orifices with cotton wool, binding head and feet, and finally shrouding the corpse in white cloth before the journey to the shrine.

But for Ali's family the diktats of religious tradition proved impossible to fulfil. 'We took the corpses home instead,' says Mohammed. 'Because they had been burned our religion prohibits us from washing them, and because we had no white cloth we felt we had no option but to bury them in the hospital bandages in which they were already wrapped.'

The number of dead also made the logistics of burial difficult. 'The *deffan* said he had two diggers, but he explained that it would take three hours to dig each grave,' says Mohammed. 'He said to me, "You have 16 dead. How can we manage? What can be done?"'

The family knew exactly what was required: they would find strength in numbers. 'We summoned all the men,' says Mohammed. 'Ali's maternal uncles, his paternal uncles, his maternal grandfather, in-laws and friends. We were 150 men.' The bodies were in such poor condition that no women were allowed to join the working party.

The men made their way to the substitute shrine they had chosen. 'It is better for Shiites, such as ourselves, if we are buried at the great shrine of Imam Ali, the cousin of our prophet Mohammed, that lies two hours south of Baghdad, in the holy city of Najaf,' explains Mohammed. Shiite Muslims, unlike Sunni Muslims, regard Imam Ali and his successors as the true, divinely inspired leaders of Islam. The Sunnis, however, do not believe that the leader of the Muslim community must be a blood relative of the prophet, and do not recognize Imam Ali as their leader.

Unfortunately, war had made the journey to the appropriate Shiite shrine impossible. The surviving family had therefore chosen the local shrine of Abu Arrooge as a substitute. By the time they arrived it was 3 p.m. and they knew they had only a few hours until darkness fell and the skies began to fill again with the sounds of terror. Such time constraints meant that more traditions had to be broken. 'If we had been at the correct shrine, we would have read the prayer that is fixed there and we would have walked around Imam Ali's grave three times, carrying the coffin as we walked; but we could not do this. Furthermore, the grave would already have been dug and the *deffan* would stand at the bottom to receive the coffin, before sliding it sideways into a cavity and bricking up the side.

'We were very afraid and we didn't know what we were doing. We had no religious man and not enough bricks, and no time to do anything but dig. We used our hands. Night was closing in and the bombing was intensifying. We were working under very difficult conditions. Some people were sent back home to look for more body pieces.'

Despite the unspeakable tragedy of the story he recounts, Mohammed is proud of the manner in which they were able to carry out this act of familial love. 'We divided into groups and we dug, and together we managed to do it in time, to dig the 16 graves before it was dark.'

Ali's grandfather Ali buried his daughter Azhar, Ali's mother. Mohammed took responsibility for Ismaeel, Ali's father. Everyone was buried in the correct manner, with their feet facing Mecca, Islam's holy city.

'I made the hole for Ismaeel and I laid Ali's arms inside upon his father's body. It was a spontaneous decision that Ali's father, as head of his family, should look after his son's two arms. Because Ismaeel's arms were curled up in front of his body, I was able to lay his son's arms underneath them.' It was almost an embrace.

As he placed Ismaeel's body into the hole he had dug, Mohammed intoned the words that he knew were vital to the well-being of the dead man on the journey that lay before him.

With tears in his eyes he said quietly, 'God is your God, Mohammed is your prophet and Ali is your *imam*. Islam is your religion. The Koran is your book. If the two angels come to question you, as surely they will, don't be afraid. Just say these words.'

Artillery fire suddenly exploded in the distance. The 16 graves were hurriedly covered in earth. Only one symbolic element remained to be completed. 'Usually a headstone is built, a monument of marble. We could not do this – we didn't even have bricks. So we pulled down palm leaves and covered the graves that way.'

And then the men hurriedly dispersed from the cemetery towards the reassuring, if insubstantial, sanctuary of their own small houses, as the sounds of warfare increased in volume in the distance. 'When I arrived home, my family asked me, "When do we say our goodbyes?" I had to explain that it was just too dangerous.'

Mohammed says he is at peace over the hasty funeral arrangements because he knows the family did all they could for their dead.

'The funeral did not take place as we would have wanted, but it was the best we could do, and better than for a lot of people. Some people are buried just near their homes because it proved impossible to take them to a shrine.

'For a while we thought that one day we might exhume Ali's family and take them to the shrine of Imam Ali, two hours away. But then we discovered that Abu Arrooge was Imam Ali's close relative, so we have decided to make it permanent and now we have peace over our decision.'

After the funeral was over, the family decided, once again, that it was too dangerous for the remaining family to stay in Baghdad. Major parts of Iraq had fallen to the coalition forces, and Baghdad, the only part of the country that had not, was now completely surrounded. 'We managed to drive the family to safety in Babylon just before the roads were closed,' says Mohammed. 'Two other members of the family went north of Baghdad, and I stayed behind.'

The family were split up and for several days could get no news of each other. Telephone networks in Baghdad were badly disrupted after repeated strikes on telephone exchanges. 'It was too dangerous for me to go to the hospital in the city centre. There was intense fighting between the Americans and Saddam's troops,' says Mohammed. He had no means of knowing whether Ali had survived.

CHAPTER EIGHT

'They Took a Photograph'

'I always knew that my parents were dead. I always knew, but nobody told me. Sometimes my Aunt Jameela would say, "I need to go away and drink a glass of water." And she'd go away and I'd hear her crying outside the room. And then when she came back I would ask her "What is it?" and she'd say, "I just went for a drink of water," but I had heard her crying and I knew why. From the very first day I drew my own conclusions.

'One day they took a photograph, but I didn't want to look at my body: I still had hope. I asked the doctors about the extent of my burning because I wanted to understand. I wanted to have the facts.'

Ali Ismaeel Abbas

Journalists had been visiting the hospital to report on civilian casualties since the bombing of Baghdad had begun. On 1 April, the day after Ali's surgery, Dr Saleh was interviewed by Jon Lee Anderson of *The New Yorker*, who quizzed him about recent war casualties. As they walked down the long hall to his office, Dr Saleh puffed on a cigarette and decided to show him the disturbing pre-operative photographs of Ali. 'It was hard to imagine that the person in the photograph could still be alive,' Anderson wrote in his feature 'War Wounds'.

Other photographs showed Ali again, on the same bed and in the same position as before, but this time without his charred appendages. Both arms had been amputated and the stumps were wrapped in white bandages. His torso was covered in some kind of clear grease. The mask had been removed from his face and he appeared to be sleeping. He had the feminine features of a pre-pubescent boy. In the final picture Ali was awake, staring at the camera with large, expressionless eyes.

Dr Saleh, a tall distinguished-looking man of 48 with a receding hairline and a polite, professional manner, told the journalist that Ali was aware he had lost his arms – he was conscious and could see the stumps – but that the boy 'had not yet acknowledged it'. Anderson asked if he could see the boy. Together, the journalist and the surgeon walked down the noisy corridors. Jon Lee Anderson asked what he was thinking about. Ali spoke for a moment in Arabic, in a boy's soft, high-pitched voice. 'He doesn't think of anything, and he doesn't remember anything,' Dr Saleh translated, explaining, in English, that Ali had not yet been told that his family were dead.

Jon Lee Anderson asked Ali about school:

He was in the sixth grade [year two] and his favourite subject was geography. As he spoke, his aunt stroked his hair. Did he like sports? Yes, he replied, especially volleyball, and also soccer. Was there anything he wanted, or needed? No, nothing. He looked at me and said something that Saleh didn't translate until I insisted: 'He says that Bush is a criminal and he is fighting for oil.' Ali had said this as he had said everything else, without expression. Ali's aunt began to sob quietly behind him. I asked Ali what he wanted to be when he grew up. 'An officer,' he said, and his aunt cried out, 'Insha'allah – If God wills it.'

On 2 April American ground forces reached the outskirts of Baghdad. The following day they took control of Saddam International Airport in the south-west of the city. For the next few days, during the last, chaotic moments of Saddam's crumbling regime, air-raids prepared the ground for troops to seize the city. Shelling intensified as countless, ear-splitting strikes were made on military and communications targets, and government buildings. F18 fighter jets dived repeatedly.

Throughout the bombardment people were being taken in their hundreds to Al-Kindi Hospital and the other front-line hospitals. Nurses were walking around in tears. The parents of injured and dying children were wailing and beating the walls in the white-tiled cubicles in the emergency ward. Three critically injured children brought to the hospital one morning had died by lunchtime.

Ali could hear the sounds of war raging outside the window. He was gripped by terrible fear for the future: all he could imagine was that he would become a childless beggar whom no woman would want to marry.

His relatives stayed by his bedside, grieving for him and praying for a solution. The morning of the operation Ali had been joined by his maternal grandfather, Ali. On the second and third day his maternal uncle Kareem looked after him. On the fourth day Kareem was replaced by Ali's aunt Jameela, who set up camp in his room and stayed for eight days. She mopped his brow with her headscarf and shooed away the flies that kept swarming on his wounds. She didn't talk much to the staff, or later the journalists, but she and Ali found strength in reading the Koran together. 'When I was feeling sad, my Aunty would say, "Well let's read a verse from the Koran," and we would read it maybe 80 times,' Ali recalls. 'The verse we read says, "Thank God that helped me and saved me. I wasn't dead. I'm not dead – I'm alive." When I was feeling low or down, sometimes we would read it all day long. It helped me a lot, and so did my religion, naturally.'

Muslims believe that the Koran is God's pure word, not an interpretation. They turn to it regularly for advice on their specific circumstances, much in the same way we might consult our astrological chart. 'We believe that good things that happen to you can turn out to be bad, but, sometimes, bad things that happen to you are for your good,' explains Ali.

On Sunday 6 April, the day before Jon Lee Anderson's story about the human cost of the war appeared on news-stands in America, a Lebanese-born journalist called Samia Nakhoul was making her daily rounds of the hospitals in Baghdad, together with Iraqi photographer Faleh Kheiber. As Gulf bureau chief of the international press agency Reuters, it was Samia's job to file copy to subscribing news organizations around the world, enabling them to keep abreast of the latest stories in the war-torn capital.

She asked one of the nurses at Al-Kindi to show her the worst case they had received. 'I wanted to know what "the worst case" meant,' she later told a journalist from *The Guardian*. The nurse told her about a burned boy. She led Samia and Faleh into the side room where Ali was lying under his rusted metal cage. 'I have covered the Lebanon war, but I had never seen anything like that,' recalls Nakhoul, who is now based in Dubai. 'I was very, very shocked. I was trying to hold myself together and not break down in front of him.'

Samia spent an hour talking to Ali and his aunt. Faleh took pictures of Ali biting his lip and trying not cry, while his aunt stroked his face with a damp rag. Fixing Samia with large brown eyes, Ali asked her a question: 'Will you help me get my arms back? If I don't get my arms back, I will commit suicide.' His plea was to become what one commentator would later describe as 'the most unbearably poignant soundbite of the war'.

'When I came out, I started sobbing like I have never sobbed in my life,' says Samia. 'I couldn't file the story for hours. I just sat and cried.' She resolved to try to persuade the International Red Cross to help Ali. Then she sat down at her computer and did her job.

When her story was ready, it travelled down the wires to newsdesks around the world: a few lines of electronic text, accompanied by a disturbing photograph, cast upon a sea of digital information being pumped out from news-agency bureaux around the world. It might well have gone unnoticed amidst so many other stories of war, but a few hours later it was spotted by Sarah Getty, news editor of the *Metro*, a London freesheet given away each morning at tube and train stations around the capital. Ali's future was about to change forever.

On Monday 7 April 2003, under the headline 'Ali, the boy who lost everything – including hope', the *Metro* published Faleh Kheiber's now famous picture of Ali on their front page; the accompanying story told how Ali planned to kill himself if he did not get new arms, and quoted his agonizing words: 'Ali Ismaeel Abbas had planned to be a soldier – now he wants to be a doctor. "But how can I?" he wept. "I don't have hands. If I don't get a pair of hands, I will commit suicide."'

At morning news conferences in every national newspaper and television newsroom in the UK, the tragedy of Ali Abbas dominated the agenda. Meanwhile, *Metro* readers, stirred by the brutally immediate photograph of Ali, were inundating the switchboard with offers of assistance. One pledged a five-figure sum to pay for his treatment. Another volunteered to adopt the boy. David Harding, a news reporter, was briefed by the news editor to find an appropriate charity to handle the donations: 'We had so many offers of help. The calls were coming in continuously,' says David. 'At this point it seemed fairly certain that Ali would die, so we needed to find a charity prepared to coordinate efforts to help other injured children in Iraq as well.'

The trail of suggestions led to a small charity based at Queen Mary's Hospital in Roehampton, west London: the Limbless Association. Staffed by people who have themselves lost arms and legs, it provides information, advice and support to Britain's 62,000 civilian amputees. David spoke to the charity's fund-raising manager, Kiera Roche. She in turn spoke to chief executive officer Diana Morgan and chairman, Zafar Khan, who says, 'We took a very rapid decision that we had to set up a fund for the treatment of Ali and children like him who'd lost limbs in the second Gulf War.'

The following morning almost every British newspaper reported the boy's heart-rending plea and published his now iconic photograph. Once again switchboards were deluged with calls from readers desperate to help. But as Samia Nakhoul's story about one war victim took on a life of its own, she herself became another. At midday on 8 April a US M1 Abrams tank stationed on a bridge across Baghdad's Tigris River swivelled its gun turret towards the Palestine Hotel, where hundreds of international journalists reporting on the conflict were billeted. A belch of flame leaped from the barrel and the entire building shook as a 120-millimetre cannon shell devastated room 1502, the Reuters suite on the fifteenth floor, killing two journalists. A piece of shrapnel sliced through Samia's skull and embedded in her brain – she was in a critical condition. Photographer Faleh Kheiber was also injured. Bundled into a blanket by her blood-spattered colleagues, Samia Nakhoul was evacuated to Kuwait for emergency surgery. She had found Ali Abbas just in time.

On 9 April 2003 Baghdad fell to American forces after 10 days of continuous bombing. Saddam Hussein's bloody 24-year reign was finally at an end, and economic sanctions could be lifted. Cheering crowds greeted American tanks as they moved into the city. Hundreds of Iraqis waved their guns above their heads and fired celebratory shots in the air. Others looted government buildings and doused effigies of Hussein in petrol. His largest statue, a six-metre tall, five-tonne bronze, was symbolically dragged with ropes from its concrete plinth in the Shahid Square of the Martyrs by jubilant young Iraqis, assisted by American soldiers in a US Marines recovery vehicle. A few moments later the ALI Fund (Ali's fund for the Limbless of Iraq) was established by the Limbless Association in London. It raised £16,000 in the first 12 hours. The following day it was launched at a press conference at the House of Commons. 'The response was phenomenal,' says the charity's chief executive, Diana Morgan. 'It started in Great Britain, and soon spread like wildfire.' As well as British donations, from coins sent in by schoolchildren to generous private cheques, money was soon arriving from Hong Kong, Japan and Australia. It seemed as if the entire world wanted to help Ali and others like him. 'There is a chance that Ali might not make it, which is why we named the fund in his honour – we hope that other Iraqi children can also be saved because of him,' Kiera Roche told journalists from her office near a large workshop where state-of-the-art artificial limbs are manufactured: just the sort of facility that could give Ali Abbas the new arms he craved.

But the focus of all this attention, 3000 kilometres away, knew nothing of the impact his words and photograph had made on televisions and in newspapers on the other side of the world. And of things such as artificial limbs he was entirely oblivious. Ali's world was a small one, filled to the brim with pain and despair. He didn't know that Baghdad had fallen to the Americans and that jubilant crowds were hurling rocks at statues nearby – only that his parents and brother were dead. He was unaware that international aid agencies had suspended their humanitarian operations in Iraq as a result of growing lawlessness. He didn't know that the door to his wing of the hospital had been locked for two days to deter looters trying to steal equipment. He could think only of his need for new arms, and his knowledge that his life would not be worth living without them.

Then two men came running into his room and grabbed his bed.

CHAPTER NINE

'Why are you Running?'

'In Baghdad there were a lot of posters and statues of Saddam, but there were always soldiers guarding them. Once I heard about a man who tried to write something on one of those pictures, some graffiti, and the soldiers took him away. Those big statues were all lies, just lies. He wasn't a good man at all. When he appeared on TV, saying, "I want to do good things for the Iraqi people," he was just making it up. All the stuff about wanting the Iraqi people to prosper was all lies as well. The salaries were very, very low, and some people who were high-ranked officers left the service and worked as taxi drivers and builders, just to avoid Saddam's system. If the Iraqi football team lost a game, then Uday, Saddam's son, would torture them for a week and they would be forced to feed horses and cattle with hay. If they won a game, they would be given a car as a present. But now that Saddam's pressure is gone the Iraqi football team play much better.'

Ali Ismaeel Abbas

On Friday 12 April, three days after Baghdad fell to US forces, Mohammed was able to visit Ali for the first time since the day after the bombing of his house, eleven days earlier. 'I didn't know if Ali would still be alive: I'd seen him and knew he was dying,' he says. 'To be honest, I had been wishing for him to die.'

Friday is traditionally a day of rest and prayers for Muslims, but at daybreak Mohammed set off on the four-hour walk to the centre of Baghdad with Ali's maternal uncle, Kareem. Mohammed had loaned his car to another relative, who was now stranded outside the city. As the men approached the outskirts of the city, they saw horrific evidence of the recent fighting. 'As American army tanks drove past us, we saw dead Iraqi soldiers buried in shallow graves behind rocks, and the burnt-out wrecks of cars, trucks and buses with dead people inside.' They witnessed the armed looters who now roamed the city's streets, stealing chairs, hat stands and ornaments from houses and shops. Government offices were also being raided, as were Saddam's palaces. A brand new combine harvester was being driven along one street. 'We saw people were carrying guns and stolen stuff, like TVs, on their shoulders. There was looting and chaos.' But even as Mohammed describes scenes of destruction and anarchy, he insists that compared to what had gone before, his city no longer felt dangerous. 'I was not afraid: there weren't any explosions and we knew the worst was over. We were happy that Saddam had gone and we thought things were about to get better. It hasn't happened, but that's what we thought at the time.'

The scene outside Al-Kindi Hospital was much more alarming: a mob shouted and the air crackled with the sound of sniper fire. On the concrete steps a security guard brandishing a rifle told Mohammed that the hospital had been occupied by militiamen, the leader of whom had donned a white doctor's gown over his traditional robe.

Where were the injured civilians now? The security guard explained that most of the seriously ill patients had been transferred during the night. Ali was now to be found at Qadissiyah Hospital, renamed Al-Sadr Hospital in the past few days. It lay in Sadr City, Baghdad's biggest workers' slum –

formerly known as Saddam City – and home to a million Shiite Muslims. After the fall of Saddam, the oppressed majority had set about renaming everything Shiite after Mohammed Al-Sadr, a religious teacher martyred by Saddam Hussein in 1999.

Realizing it was by now too late to walk to Baghdad's north-eastern suburbs, Mohammed reluctantly turned around and thumbed a lift home. He still had no news of the boy.

On Tuesday 8 April Al-Kindi Hospital had been capably managing mass casualties. Two days later it had been desecrated – attacked and looted in the orgy of lawlessness that swept across Baghdad as US troops captured the city. A few hours before the looters forced their way inside on Wednesday afternoon, a decision was taken by the doctors to evacuate the hospital. The raiders had already made several attempts to breach hospital security and were growing increasingly aggressive. Caring for critically ill patients like Ali had become impossible. Many patients were evacuated to Al-Sadr Hospital, most making the painful journey by double-decker bus, but Ali remembers being taken by ambulance: 'The doctor of the ambulance came running into my room with another man. The ambulance man was saying about me, "I'm not leaving this hospital without him. I have to take him with me." They were running very, very quickly,' remembers Ali. 'I asked them "Why are you running?" and they said, "People are trying to break in: I am running fast to get you to safety." We were moved to the other hospital because of the stealing that was going on. My aunty was in such a hurry that she mixed up the plastic bags that were our luggage with those of another boy who came with us in that ambulance. He was 16 or 17 and had lost an eye and a leg.'

A few hours after Ali was evacuated, Al-Kindi Hospital was stripped of everything that could be moved, including the light fittings. Water supplies donated to the hospital by charity workers were a major target as were beds, medical equipment and the scant supplies of medicine. Some of the stolen items were brazenly driven away by ambulance. Journalists reported that looters could also be seen walking the streets with X-ray machines. Only two doctors remained, but with no equipment they could offer little more than first-aid advice. The International Red Cross described conditions at Al-Kindi as 'chaotic and catastrophic'. East of central Baghdad the Al-Rashad psychiatric hospital was torched and more than a thousand patients, many of them unstable, were turned into the streets.

Meanwhile, in the UK the photograph of the little boy and his desperate appeal for new arms was being widely referred to as 'a symbol of the human tragedy of the war in Iraq'. Aware of a growing public hunger for more information about the boy in the picture, editors urged their foreign correspondents to find him. Word soon got around the close-knit community of journalists in Baghdad that Ali Abbas had been moved. And so they came, and stood helplessly by Ali's bedside able to do little more than report his despair. On 12 April Dr Hussein Al-Atabi, a hospital paediatrician, told Philip Sherwell of *The Sunday Telegraph*, 'To be honest, it is probably better if he dies. I don't want it, but that's the awful truth. He has no arms and terrible burns. His physical suffering is enormous and the psychological damage will be immense. We are treating him with the most advanced antibiotics we have. But he needs a specialist burns centre and there is nothing like that here now.'

Within days of Samia Nakhoul's report several British newspapers had started appeals to raise funds for Ali and others like him. 'Ali was not from any affluent or particularly well-educated family, yet he was able to articulate himself in a strong and confident way, way beyond his years,' said Piers Morgan, the editor of the *Daily Mirror*, during a television interview. 'It was a phenomenal human story, one of the biggest of the year.' The *Daily Mirror* initially raised money for Unicef and helped rebuild a school in southern Iraq, but began printing the Limbless Association's appeal details in August. The *Evening Standard* contacted the British Red Cross. *The Times* also started to publicize details of the Limbless Association's appeal, as did several other broadsheets and broadcasters including GMTV. Within days donations to the ALI Fund had reached £50,000. Web sites and online discussion forums were created, including one on the Limbless Association's site where hundreds of messages of support and concern were posted daily.

As Ali's plight was discussed around the world, everyone wanted to help him. The problem was that no-one knew how. Al-Sadr Hospital, now the only functioning hospital in Baghdad, was under attack from looters and rogue militias. And impoverished Sadr City, where the hospital was located, was a volatile and lawless neighbourhood that was becoming increasingly dangerous in the wake of Saddam's downfall. There had been no public services or police during peacetime – now the streets boiled with smoke and gunfire.

For help on Ali's behalf journalists approached aid agencies working in Iraq, but were told it was considered too unsafe for them to enter Sadr City. Several reporters made enquiries with local US military contacts. To no avail. Ali was effectively under siege. All that the newspapers could do was continue to print addresses for their various appeals and publish emotive editorials demanding government intervention for the injured innocents.

On Thursday 10 April the BBC broadcast a moving news report about Ali in which his doctors said they feared time could be running out for him. 'His burns are so severe he risks septicaemia unless he is taken to a hospital with advanced intensive care,' they said. Diana Morgan, chief executive of the Limbless Association, remembers that immediately following the broadcast the phones at the charity 'went into meltdown' as five full-time staff and several volunteers struggled to cope with the volume of calls. 'People began pleading with us to do something to get him out of there. I remember this appalling feeling of impotence. We had raised all this money in his name, but with the airspace around the hospital controlled by the Americans we couldn't yet do anything tangible for him.'

The Red Cross and Unicef were experiencing similar pressure from the general public. 'It is true that during any conflict or disaster an image that reflects the wider horror of the situation can engage the public at a deeper level. This just happens,' said Sir Nicholas Young, chief executive of the British Red Cross, and David Bull, director of Unicef UK, in a letter to *The Daily Telegraph* on 19 April.

During the Vietnam War the pitiful image of a naked nine-year-old girl called Kim Phuc defined and helped to end a war. A Vietnamese press photographer, Nick Ut, witnessed the devastating napalm strike upon the village of Trang Bang on 8 June 1972, the result of a fatal mistake by the American-funded South Vietnamese army. As the smoke cleared he saw a little girl, whose clothes had been incinerated from her body by napalm burning at 1200 degrees centigrade, running from the chaos and flames – and into the eye of history. After Nick Ut pressed the shutter, Kim Phuc carried on running, towards soldiers and journalists and into a future that would be forever marked by that instant in time. Today she is a mother of two living in Canada, an ambassador for Unesco and the founder of the Kim Foundation to help child victims of war. 'For a long time I wanted to build a normal life,' she says, 'but then I realized that this is a very powerful image and I now choose to work with that for ever.' She explains that she has chosen to see 'that little girl' running and crying out, not as a cry of pain but as a cry for peace.

Ali was just one of many seriously injured child victims in Al-

Sadr Hospital. Lying two floors away from him was 11-year-old Fouad Abu Haidar, who had lost his left arm when a missile struck his house. There was also a three-year-old boy with a fractured skull, a 12-year-old girl who had lost a leg, a nine-year-old whose foot had been blown off, and a small girl wounded by shrapnel that had ripped through her abdomen into her spleen. Many children had been killed outright. Why had Ali become the focus of such collective desperation when there were so many other seriously injured children throughout Iraq?

Psychologist Susan Quilliam believes we are primed to focus our attention on a single victim in this way: 'When we had friends and family on the front line in war time, we didn't feel guilty. We got directly involved instead. Now that we are observers of wars, rather than active participants, our overriding emotion is guilt.' She says that both men and women are physiologically wired to want to protect children. 'Seizing on a single innocent casualty allows us to reclaim our humanity and absolve our guilt. We can discuss his or her plight with our friends, and share our compassion without compromising any sense of loyalty to our armed forces.'

And, with advances in the media, it is no longer enough that a child should look innocent: he should sound innocent as well. 'We saw the powerful photograph of Kim Phuc, but we never heard what she had to say,' says Quilliam. 'We not only saw Ali Abbas; we also heard his clearly articulated cry for help as well – this was a very powerful combination.'

Diana Morgan of the Limbless Association felt a deep personal connection to the little boy who had been filmed pleading for new arms. On Thursday 9 August 1990, during the run-up to the first Gulf War, Diana lost both her legs when she fell beneath a slam-door train that pulled away as she was stepping aboard at London's Wandsworth Common station. 'I had one foot on the running board and as I raised the other the train jerked ferociously. It was moving and I wasn't on. One foot slipped, my hands reached for the door frame, the train jolted again. One leg dropped below the running board, into the gap between the train and platform. I fell slowly, trying to save myself. Then 400 tons of metal began to move against my back.' Fear shrieked in her brain as she felt herself being tugged along and dragged down.

'Losing my legs was like dying,' explains this tall, empathetic and sincere woman. 'But gradually I was able to reinvent it all.' Diana is an inspiring example of the independence amputees can attain. Three years after the near-fatal accident she gave birth to her beautiful daughter, Lara. She has also chaired the PTA at her daughter's London school and, until recently, worked in TV development and production. Her decision to apply for the post of chief executive officer of the Limbless Association in February was serendipitous: Diana Morgan took up the new role on 31 March 2003 – just a few hours after the happy life of the then unknown Ali Abbas was decimated by a stray missile.

'I'd expected to settle gently into the job: then Ali's photograph was published. It took me right back to being under that train for 40 minutes. Here was this orphaned child lying in intensive care without any anaesthetic, trying to stop himself from crying, having lost both his arms. There was something about the look in his eyes. I have never, ever seen courage like his. I'd had the benefit of the best pain control, one of the world's leading surgical teams and my family by my bedside, yet I could well remember the terrible desolation I felt as I tried to take in what had happened to my legs. It is difficult to conceive of the particular significance of losing your arms – you can't cuddle anyone ever again – and he had also lost the two people who could most have wanted to cuddle him.'

Ali and Diana may be from very different cultures, but she knew without a doubt that this young Arabic-speaking boy needed the assistance of people who had gone through similar emotions, whether they spoke the same language or not. 'As an amputee, I knew I was closer than many other people to understanding how helpless he would be feeling,' she explains. 'I also knew that the Limbless Association could offer Ali a special kind of support.' But first the charity had to join the fight to get Ali specialized medical attention outside the war-zone.

With the pain of her own memories acting as a catalyst, Diana was soon working around the clock on Ali's behalf, along with the chairman Zafar Khan and their colleagues. Countless calls were made to Downing Street, the White House and the Foreign Office, as the team coped simultaneously with a blizzard of media enquiries and the sustained deluge of donations.

On Sunday 13 April 2003 Andrea Catherwood, ITN's international correspondent, stood by Ali's bedside, shocked to the core. Embedded at the start of the war with the forward helicopter unit of the RAF, this veteran of Afghanistan, Kosovo, Sierra Leone and Albania had recently left the unit to get a more independent perspective. She had been in Baghdad for a few days when ITN asked her to find Ali in this now lawless city of gun battles and spiralling anarchy. Half an hour later she and her cameraman and producer were driving through militia barricades in Baghdad's poorest area en route to Al-Sadr Hospital. Andrea thought she'd reported from enough war-zones to know what to expect. In Afghanistan she had herself been injured when a suicide bomber blew himself up with a grenade just 10 metres away from her, leaving a piece of shrapnel so deeply embedded in her knee that her surgeon refused to remove it.

'People were shooting constantly at the hospital, trying to break it down, to ready it for looting. Snipers were using the roof as a vantage point. There was an extremely dangerous atmosphere there. Baghdad was one of the most lawless places I've ever been sent, worse even than Afghanistan. There were so many men firing guns indiscriminately. But even with all that going on I'm ashamed to say that my first instinct was to recoil in horror from the scale of Ali's wounds,' she says.

'I've seen a lot of injured children, too many dead bodies, but never anything like this. His wounds were decaying and the smell was overpowering. I didn't think this poor child, in such enormous pain and so badly mutilated, could possibly survive. You would expect that a child in this condition would be on a drip, being constantly monitored, but there was none of that. Once a day he was washed. That seemed to be the sum total of his treatment.

'To me, what seemed to set Ali apart was that he'd had the worst of everything – he'd lost both arms and his parents – and managed to survive. We filmed so many other injured children, the scale of suffering was hard to take in. Hundreds of children had lost an arm or a leg, been burned or lost a parent. Perhaps people find it hard to relate to endless images of suffering, because it was just one child who seemed to capture the public's attention.

'At this stage I don't think the doctors were thinking about getting him taken out; they were trying instead to show us what the bomb had done. I stood there with my cameraman and a local translator and felt we should retreat: it was just too awful. But then I looked at Ali's face and eyes, the one part of him that wasn't horribly maimed and injured, and suddenly, rather than seeing him as this atrocity of war, I saw this little boy.' With the help of her interpreter, she began to talk to him, and stayed by his side for the rest of the afternoon.

Later, on the hospital steps, surrounded by the feverish crowd, she filed an emotive news report that crystallized her feelings of hopelessness: 'You can't hold him or hug him. You can't even touch his skin. You can just ruffle his hair and feel angry and impotent ... Dead bodies on the forecourt, militia at the gates, and yet this hospital is the best that Baghdad has to offer. This war that destroyed Ali's family has also destroyed any chance he had of getting proper medical care in his own country.'

There was a further complication: although Ali's story had dominated the UK news agenda for nearly a week, he was still unknown in the United States. 'The story about Ali didn't break in the US until after the bombing was already over, 11 days after he was injured,' says the American doctor, April Hurley, who had tried without success to get pictures of Ali published there after she first saw him in Al-Kindi Hospital. 'We were attempting to get his story out in the US, but publication of the casualty pictures was delayed there, even though every other story was immediately reported. The mainstream media justified why they didn't show the civilian casualties – they didn't think they were tasteful enough to show the audience.'

All that was about to change as Andrea Catherwood's report on Ali was picked up by CNN, America's influential 24-hour news channel. Soon he was all over the US news networks. Ali had become an international sensation – perhaps something could now be done to rescue him? Among those who saw the CNN newscast was Fayez Omar, a director of the World Bank who was based in South Africa. At the time of the broadcast he was in Washington D.C. He discussed the boy's plight with a contact of his, an American senator, who, in turn, undertook to contact America's central command centre in Qatar in a bid to try to pressure the US military to get Ali out of Iraq. 'On Saturday 12 April, the Limbless Association got a call from Fayez Omar to say that the Americans hoped to evacuate Ali from Iraq to their military base in Kuwait on 15 or 16 April,' says Diana Morgan. 'We were told to provisionally book an International SOS plane to evacuate Ali from Kuwait to the UK, should it be required.' Diana then phoned the head of ITV News and asked for a message to be passed on to Andrea Catherwood: 'Please tell Ali, help is hopefully on its way.'

Ali's story had also made an impact in the neighbouring State of Kuwait, where the government had received eight critically ill Iraqi child victims of the war since the start of the conflict. Dr Ahmad Al-Shatti, the director of Health Education and the Media Department at Kuwait's Ministry of Health, was one of those who saw the CNN broadcast. 'I was watching the late-night news and Ali's story made a huge impact on me,' he recalls. At the Minister of Health's daily briefing the following morning, Ali Abbas dominated the agenda for three-quarters of an hour. 'Everyone was talking about him, and by the end of the meeting there was consensus that if it was possible for the Alliance to evacuate him to Kuwait, that we would treat him,' says Dr Al-Shatti.

The difficulty that all Ali's would-be saviours faced was that, unlike the other rescued children, he was trapped in a part of Iraq that was not yet under coalition control. The north-eastern suburb of Baghdad was just too dangerous for the US military to enter.

CHAPTER TEN

'He Will Die if he Stays'

'The summer is fishing season. I go with my friends to the Diyala River near my house. I was nine or ten when I started to fish. We catch a lot of fish of all sizes. The biggest one I ever caught was 30 centimetres long! We take the fish home and eat them. My family love fish. I had a rod ... but sometimes the rods float away and then we start trying to fish with our hats, though we have more success using plastic bags. During the season, which is one month a year, the fish become very abundant. Sometimes I take my doggies with me. I've got plenty of them: I've got a doggy called Rio, another called Addouna and one called Theed. Sometimes the doggies try to catch fish with their mouths; sometimes they use their paws. Sometimes they just go to the plastic bags where the catch is and steal them, you know!

'I love animals, but my favourite of all is little chicks. We used to have plenty of chickens and chicks, but we don't like to eat our own chickens: they are too nice. Instead, we play with them and they lay us eggs and stuff. When I go to feed the chickens, I'd say, "Teet! Teet! Teet!" We just like to have them there, you see.'

Ali Ismaeel Abbas

On 13 April, the day after his fruitless visit to Al-Kindi Hospital in central Baghdad, Mohammed was driven to Al-Sadr Hospital from Za'Faraniya by Ali's uncle, Hamza. If Ali was still alive, Mohammed planned to take Aunt Jameela's place at his bedside – she hadn't seen her family for days.

As he drew nearer to Sadr City, on a divided highway full of cars moving erratically, he could see the Ministry of Oil and the Ministry of Transport being ransacked by men and boys. He saw the skeletal ruins of the Iraqi Olympic Committee headquarters, where Uday Hussein used to torture athletes as an incentive to excel. It had been bombed and looted. Men in headscarves were standing on traffic circles and in the central reservation, toting automatic weapons and carrying anti-tank rockets. One British foreign correspondent remarked that it looked more like Beirut or Mogadishu than a city under American control.

At 10 a.m. Mohammed arrived at Al-Sadr Hospital to find staff barricading the gates as dozens of people, some ill, some seemingly healthy, tried to force their way inside. Angry crowds swirled outside as lorries unloaded ever more casualties of sniper fire. Mohammed struggled to get past the volunteer guards brandishing Kalashnikov rifles. 'A guard inspected me to check I wasn't carrying explosives. I told him that my family had died and I had relatives inside the hospital.' He was sent to explain his case to Shiite cleric Sheikh Kathim Al-Fartousi, who had been delegated by his religious school to protect the hospital – to the consternation of some of the doctors, who felt that hospitals should remain under secular control. This bearded priest, dressed in white headdress, black robes and grey tunic, had gathered together a small army of his students. Armed with long knives and rifles, they now patrolled the hospital grounds and roamed the wards and corridors in an attempt to stop the looters striking there too.

'When I mentioned Ali's name, this talkative, authoritative man surprised me: he knew who Ali was. He said that the media had been visiting him and "disturbing everything". What was all this about? He talked of broken promises. You could tell from his attitude that he was used to getting his way.'

Inside, Al-Sadr Hospital was experiencing the same problems as the Al-Kindi. The cleaners had fled days before. So, too, had many of the doctors and nurses, too frightened to continue their work against the backdrop of a city spiralling into anarchy where looting and shooting were widespread, or willing but unable to get to the hospitals due to the scenes of chaos on the streets outside. The overstretched hospital was admitting only the worst cases. More than 300 patients were being tended by just 22 doctors and a nursing staff at a third of its capacity. 'People were trying to come in and steal stuff and loot things,' remembers Ali.

Mohammed found him lying in a soiled bed, under a neon light, in a room with broken windows. The boy's head, wrapped in a white bandage, was resting on a red and brown pillow. A pink polyester blanket lay over his chipped metal cage. He was moaning with pain, and his blistered, melted skin had begun to smell. Flies swarmed over his wounds, and Mohammed tried to shoo them away. Aunt Jameela was there and so was the small crowd of concerned-looking Westerners with cameras that he'd been told about. Gunshots could be heard outside. The whitewashed walls were dirty; there was water on the floor. It was yet another filthy side room in another chaotic hospital where the only certainty was that the skin-graft surgery Ali needed to survive was a logistical impossibility. 'A number of journalists were concentrating on Ali,' says Mohammed. 'One of them introduced herself as Andrea Catherwood from Britain's ITN and told me that she wanted to help Ali, perhaps to send him to Jordan.'

The medical staff agreed that his only possible hope of

survival lay in being taken out of the country. Even then they only estimated the odds of his recovery at one in two. 'You have seen one Ali, but there are thousands of Alis in this city,' one doctor at Al-Sadr told *The Times*. 'He has been promised so much, but he will die before those promises are fulfilled.'

Ali urgently needed to be evacuated to a sanitary environment in a hospital with advanced intensive-care facilities, but he was too unwell to make a long journey by road. His only hope was a mercy airlift organized by the military. Caroline Spelman MP, then Shadow Secretary of State for International Development (who would later join the six-person committee of the Limbless Association's ALI Fund with fellow MPs Jenny Tonge and Tony Colman) was acutely aware of the complexities in bringing him out: 'A burns victim is very, very vulnerable,' she told the BBC. 'He has to be in a stable condition and it has to be safe to transport him.'

A doctor explained to Ali's concerned uncle that the greatest threat to Ali's survival were the bacteria now breeding rampantly on the surface of his open wounds: 'His life is in danger. Every burns patient is prone to infection. And infection can cause septic shock, which can cause all the body to fail at any moment.' Each moment Ali remained in a non-sterile environment increased the risk of septicaemia. Infection of the blood leads to major organ failure – it can kill within hours. So it was only by repeated scrubbing of Ali's weeping wounds that the nursing team had any chance of delaying this inevitability. But there was no medicine to diminish the pain of this procedure. As increasingly anarchic crowds celebrated the fall of a dictator, Ali's sisters prayed over his burned body and sobbed as they heard his screams when he was washed. Time was running out for their little brother. Ali's dedicated nurse, Fatin Sharhad, noticed with dismay that his pockets of infection were growing larger by the day. She and her colleague Karim had devoted themselves to caring for their most vulnerable patient.

'Fatin said she was only coming to the hospital because she wanted to look after me,' says Ali. 'She said if I left the hospital she wouldn't be coming in any more. She used to send her children to play and sit with me. Another time, Karim told me, "I have come to the hospital because of you."'

Like many other employees working within the fallen regime, Fatin and Karim had not been paid for a fortnight. Fatin's soldier husband, Talal, had not been seen for 10 days. There was no-one to look after her young sons, so they went with her on ward rounds. Every day she saw helicopters and aircraft flying over the city, but was perplexed. Why hadn't they come for Ali? Despite her own problems Fatin decided to write a letter, with the help of a *Daily Mirror* journalist, to the two most important men in the world. If they couldn't help Ali, no-one could.

Dear Mr Prime Minister and Mr President,
My name is Fatin. I am a nurse since 1990 when I graduated from the Rofaida nursing school in Baghdad but I am not a specialist in burns. I need a doctor who knows about burns but there isn't one here. I do my best but I do not know how exactly I should be nursing this boy or what drugs to give him. But there is no-one else, so it is me who must try to look after him. Many journalists have visited Ali and taken his picture, but still he is here. The situation is desperate. He will die if he stays. Please send one of your helicopters or planes to take him away. You have all this technology to bomb us, to make the missile that burned Ali's house. But you cannot spare one aircraft for one day to save a life? I don't know if you know about Ali, but I hope you do. He is a beautiful boy who has lost all his family and now his arms. Do you know how it feels to be a nurse and to have to watch a child dying in front of you when there is a chance he could be saved?

As I write this today, Ali is sleeping. He is still alive but every day his condition deteriorates. Unless we get him away he will die from blood poisoning. His wounds will become more and more infected. We have no planes or helicopters – but you do.

Please Sirs, I ask you from the bottom of my heart to help us.

Yours,

Fatin Mhssin Sharhad

Her letter was published in the *Daily Mirror* the following day, Monday 14 April, together with editorial calls from the paper for Tony Blair to intervene in Ali's case. The boy's plight had so far moved *Daily Mirror* readers to raise £95,000 for him and other young victims. That afternoon, during Prime Minister's Questions, Tony Blair responded. 'We will do whatever we can to help him and others in similar situations. Within the past 24 hours, two Iraqi children have been flown out to the UK for medical treatment, but they were both from inside our area of control. We are working with the US forces to do what we can for Ali and others,' he said. Although it is not RAF policy to airlift civilians to British hospitals, exceptions had been made for two burns victims from villages near Basra. Raeed Amar, 14, had been flown to Birmingham Children's Hospital suffering from 85 per cent burns, after a bomb in his village set fire to a stash of cans of cooking oil stockpiled by villages before the war. Horrifically burned from head to foot, he was left with virtually no skin and had been taken unconscious to a field hospital, requiring urgent life-saving treatment (Raeed died on 4 May 2003). Six-month-old Mareyam Ailan, badly burned on her face and arms in a domestic fire in Basra, was given life-saving aid at Liverpool's Alder Hey Children's Hospital after her parents contacted British soldiers.

However, because Baghdad was under American, not British,

control, the British Army could not intervene. Furthermore, Downing Street emphasized that helping Ali was further complicated because Sadr City was still not deemed safe enough for the American military to enter. A spokesman for the Prime Minister explained that there were security concerns with flying the boy out of Iraq or sending a team to care for him. Saddam's reign of terror may have ended, but Ali was still trapped in hostile territory. As anarchy reigned in Baghdad, Ali's fate lay in the hands of the US army. Could he survive long enough?

Under Saddam's regime Iraq's borders had been closed. Now it seemed possible that Ali might leave the country of his birth for the first time in his life. His family understood that there was a risk he would leave their protective embrace and die on foreign soil, but they also knew that this was his only chance of survival. It was clear that he was going to need an exceptional consort on this daunting journey. Muslim tradition dictates that in the event of the death of both parents, any surviving children become the responsibility of their eldest paternal uncle. But Ismaeel's brother was an old man and not healthy enough to take on such responsibility. Mohammed was clearly most suitable: he was intelligent, personable and spoke a small amount of English. He had also had a very close relationship with Ismaeel; everyone knew that they had been good friends as well as first cousins. Mohammed is also a first cousin to Ali's maternal grandfather, and brother to Ali's stepmother. A wise and responsible man, with a handsome face and confiding manner, Mohammed Abd Hamza exudes an air of quiet nobility. His hair and moustache have silvered to a distinguished grey. He seems at least a decade older than his 37 years. This gentle, affectionate man was just the sort of surrogate parent Ali most needed by his side.

Mohammed agreed that he was the most appropriate guardian for Ali. He would miss his family, but he owed this act of love to Ali and his father. 'I treated Ali how I would have treated his father, Ismaeel, by being a close and loving friend.'

He started arranging Ali's sheets each day after they had been washed. He kissed his cheeks and fed him thin soup.

On Monday 14 April, the morning after her first news report, Andrea returned to the hospital to visit Ali. She brought him a packet of chocolates. 'I was feeding him Smarties because he was existing on something that looked a bit like brown gruel, and he was very weak. They seemed to cheer him up a bit, but you could see that moving was agony for him – even lifting his head to swallow was painful. I talked to him a little bit about football and he told me he liked David Beckham. Part of me thought, "You star." Suddenly I could see just a glimmer of hope.'

She spent several hours with him that day, in between working on other stories. 'I spent a lot of time gazing at him, and I drew him cartoons of footballers. He told me his sister liked drawing, so I started drawing whatever I could think of. I wanted to help distract him from the long hours of just lying there in agony, but I was conscious of not getting his hopes up too much, however. I tried to explain to Mohammed that I desperately wanted to help, but that I couldn't make the Americans come. I also thought there was a very good chance that they wouldn't come. It's easy to look back and say, "There's a famous kid. Why didn't they take him?" but at the time he wasn't so well known.'

She senses that it must have been difficult for Ali and his family to see Westerners and not understand why they weren't solving the problem. 'I wouldn't have expected Ali to work out who we all were, what roles we all fulfilled,' she says. 'At one point he told me that he hated being washed, but I didn't really know why at that stage.' In the afternoon, just as Andrea was leaving, a doctor came in with a trolley on to which he moved Ali, who was by now sobbing uncontrollably.

At 8.30 a.m. the following morning, Tuesday 15 April, Andrea Catherwood returned to the hospital to visit Ali once more. 'The local militia were taking an interest in Ali's case and Mohammed had told them I was helping him, so they let me in.' As on the previous day, she took no camera to his bedside.

'All day Ali was saying to me, "When are the Americans coming?" He'd obviously overheard a discussion between the doctors since I was last there. He kept thinking he was hearing a helicopter and would ask me, "Is the helicopter coming?" He said repeatedly that he didn't want to be washed and he hoped the Americans would come before that time. He was trying to seek assurance, in fact, that he would never have to be washed again.'

But by 5.30 p.m., as the light began to fade, there was no sign of the Americans. One of the nurses who had noticed the growing rapport between the glamorous journalist and the small boy, asked Andrea for her assistance. Ali's daily wash could no longer be delayed.

'Mohammed had been helping wash him every day up till then, but he told me he couldn't bear to do it again,' says Andrea. 'The nurse's actual words to me were, "Please, will you come and hold him down?" Ali was begging me not to let this happen to him. He was saying, "Please don't let them do this to me." I did not know what I was letting myself in for.'

Ali was wheeled out of the side ward down to a toilet area for his wounds to be washed. The tiles there were filthy, cracked and covered with specks of blood. While one nurse attached an old piece of hose to a dripping cold water tap, his colleague carefully unwrapped Ali's amputations. Andrea was appalled at what she saw. 'The remains of arteries and veins were clearly visible,' she says.

Ali's burns were sprayed with cold water. And then the scrubbing began. The task went on this occasion to a young doctor, aware he had to remove the dead top layer in an effort to prevent infection – it was the only way to stop Ali contracting septicaemia. This vital but unpalatable treatment meant interfering directly with live tissue. There was no anaesthetic. Ali's skin was completely raw – this was not so much washing, as torture.

'I thought Ali simply didn't like being washed, that I was being asked to distract him. How wrong I was. It became obvious that my role was to help prevent him from moving while his wounds were scrubbed. My job was to hold his head.

'He was wriggling and screaming and the pain was so bad he began to vomit,' Andrea says, shuddering at the memory. 'Ali tried to hold eye contact with me. Then he lost consciousness. I might have been crying as I concentrated on returning his gaze; I can't remember. We had to do horrible things.' She was vaguely aware of the nurses apologizing to her at what they were being forced to do.

Treating Ali took its toll on all who cared for him. Moments after he was delivered back to his room, Andrea found the young medic who had been the scrubber that day, weeping against a wall. She put her arm around him. 'He couldn't believe he had to put a child through this,' says Andrea. 'The medical staff were distraught. I didn't know it was possible to suffer that much pain and live. I will never forget what I saw,' she says.

Mohammed concurs: 'The experience of watching Ali being washed is something I will never forget,' he says. 'They had to wash him or he would die, but there were times when they had to trim the flesh ...' His eyes fill with tears as he remembers being forced to hold the little boy still during this horrific process. 'There was no medicine, no treatment, but occasionally the Muslim cleric who was guarding the hospital, Sheikh Al-Fartousi, would come up and put a packet of painkillers in my hand. They weren't able to provide much at all, so I was always asked to keep it safe. Now Ali has developed a phobia of being washed. Every day is a battle, but we get there.'

As the afternoon of 15 April wore on, Andrea felt increasingly dismayed that help had still not arrived. She knew she would soon have to leave in order to get back to her hotel before darkness, when the roads became unsafe, but she was determined to do something more for Ali. 'I realized I had to try and prevent him being put through the torture of being washed another day. I set off from the hotel, saying, "I'm going to go and get the Americans." Later I cried buckets.'

As she left the hospital, still too shocked to cry, she recorded a short statement to camera: 'The American military had said they would take Ali out today on a medical flight to Kuwait, but the sun is setting now and there's still no sign of them.'

Fortunately, thanks to an Australian journalist and his Kuwaiti-based interpreter, everything was already in place.

As they bumped along a gravel track heading north across the Kuwaiti desert towards the Iraqi border, Peter Wilson and photographer John Feder spent a few moments questioning the wisdom of their decision. Trying to get into the war-zone as unilateral journalists was one thing. Doing so by attempting to drive 160 kilometres across the desert in a hired rental car was quite another, even if they were frustrated by having spent 11 fruitless days in Kuwait City trying to get official documentation. They couldn't use the main highway north. 'The Kuwaitis and coalition were keeping the media off it,' says Peter. Hence their unorthodox approach. 'I wanted to report on the people's war, not the soldiers' war. That's why I wanted to remain unembedded,' explains Peter, a bespectacled 43-year-old Australian, who has worked for his country's national daily paper, *The Australian*, since 1991.

The flat wastes that lie between the emirate and southern Iraq are featureless and disorientating, with no sealed roads but plenty of criss-crossing vehicle tracks. The only means the journalists had of checking their location was the GPS connection on the satellite phone supplied by their employer. 'We knew from maps that we had to go due north, so we would stop, take our map references with the GPS system, mark that spot on a map, then drive for ten minutes and do another reading to confirm our direction.' It took the paper's European correspondent and the photographer just four hours to reach the Iraqi border 113 kilometres north of Kuwait City where they were promptly turned back by British and Kuwaiti soldiers.

Two days later, on 26 March 2003, three days before the stray missile devastated Ali's home and the day after British forces began fighting Iraqi militia in Basra, they tried again. This time they were passengers in a more appropriate vehicle, a four-wheel-drive Mitsubishi Pajero driven by their newly hired 'fixer' and translator, Stewart Innes. With a Lebanese mother and a Scottish father, this Arabic-speaking resident of Kuwait was destined to become a key player, along with Peter Wilson, in the story of the as yet uninjured Ali Abbas. As a 'fixer' – a man essential in keeping foreign journalists alive, yet who knows where the action is – Innes would soon prove himself invaluable.

Peter's second attempt at the border was successful. 'We managed to tag on the back end of an enormous coalition convoy and bluff our way through the border,' he says. They had joined the supply line, delivering troops, supplies, weapons and vehicles to front-line forces in Iraq. Once across the border, the journalists peeled away and went to ground. They spent the next five nights near Umm Qasr, 40 minutes from Basra, 'roaming around': interviewing by day, and sleeping by the roadside at night. It was dangerous work. On Monday 31 March – as Ali Abbas lay in Al-Kindi Hospital lamenting his lost arms and lost life – Peter, Stewart and John were captured by Fedayeen gunmen, a militia loyal to Saddam Hussein, one of whom was wearing an olive green uniform of the Ba'ath Party. 'I really thought we were in trouble,' says Peter. 'We had guns shoved in our faces, and it looked like we were being taken to the river, not into town. I thought we were going to be shot, but then we arrived at a Ba'ath Party station where we were interrogated and locked up for the night. They were intimidating, but very proper. A few small things went missing, but we had thousands of US dollars in cash, laptops, cameras and flak jackets – which would have been very attractive to them at that particular time – but none of that was stolen. They were very keen to show that the rule of law applied in Iraq. Once they accepted that we were journalists, not spies, our offence was having broken visa laws.'

The following day they were driven north to Baghdad by their nervous captors. 'John and I were in our Pajero with an Iraqi driver and two guards carrying AK47s. Stewart was in another car with a driver and a guard,' says Peter. Bizarrely, their captors chose to drive straight through the battlefield. Out of the dirty car windows Peter could see manoeuvring Abrams tanks dug into the dirt, while Apache helicopter gunships hovered menacingly. 'Tanks were exploding all around us. Even the men driving us were terrified,' he says.

Once at the Hotel Palestine in central Baghdad, they were placed under house arrest. Eight days later the city fell to US forces and their minders fled. 'We reclaimed our confiscated equipment and were soon up and reporting,' says Peter.

Three days later, on 12 April, they visited a prison to report on the desperate relatives who were trying to locate their loved ones following the fall of Saddam. Then they drove to the ransacked house of Saddam's son Uday. Their final destination was Al-Sadr Hospital. 'I was interested in the Shiite clerics who had organized their own militia to protect the hospital. We finished off with an interview with the hospital's Christian director, Dr Mowafak Gorea. By then it was getting near curfew, but he prevailed upon us to interview the families of several wounded kids. At the end he asked if we wanted to see Ali.

'Only two people were allowed in his room, and I sent the photographer to take his picture, and Stewart, the interpreter, to talk to him. I didn't want to write about how heartbroken I was. My view was that Ali didn't need me trying to form a bond with him. But as the door opened he was looking straight at me. I instinctively smiled and lifted a hand to wave, forgetting myself, and then he smiled and raised his stump towards me, before turning away.'

When Stewart came out, his eyes were red. 'I asked Ali whether he was in pain, and he told me, "My mother died; my father died. Who will help me? What will they do? When are they coming to help me?" All these journalists had been saying they were going to get him out. His room was not sterile at all. He was very susceptible to infections. They didn't have any morphine, so he was also in constant pain.'

Later that night Peter filed his story about the militia clerics and mentioned Ali, in passing, near the end of his article. Published in Australia later that day, Peter's words were illustrated with John's photo, the latest to be taken of the boy. The following day a Perth property developer called Tony Trevisan contacted the offices of *The Australian* and offered to help Ali. 'I called him back on my satellite phone and said, "I'm sure he's fine: half the world's press are trying to help him. But if you want to send some money, I'll try to find out where you can send it."'

Peter returned to the hospital that afternoon. 'I'd had a difficult time lately and had had enough of journalism for a while.' He is referring to the fact that he had cradled one of the victims of the Palestine Hotel bombing, a Ukrainian cameraman called Taras Protsyuk, as he lay dying after the shell attack had obliterated the Reuters suite five days earlier. 'I was still a bit shocked. I'd stayed on my knees in the room, my hands and forearms covered in blood, until Rageh Omaar of the BBC made me get out of the room for fear of a second attack. Rather than writing more stories until leaving Baghdad, I was happy to see if we could do something good instead.'

When he and Stewart returned to the hospital on 13 April to tell Mohammed about Perth businessman Tony Trevisan's offer of financial assistance, the director of the hospital Dr Mowafak Gorea was not happy to see them. 'He was tired and he turned on me, saying, "You journalists are all liars. You all make promises, but none of you keep them." It turned out that two days earlier, a few hours after I'd interviewed him, he had attended a meeting at the Palestine Hotel with US Navy Petty Officer Ed Martin, a member of the US Marines. The meeting had been brokered by a British journalist, but it hadn't gone well. The Americans had wanted to help but didn't know how; they had a whole city falling apart,' says Peter. 'The proposal put forward by the journalist was for the marines to evacuate Ali to a nearby US hospital ship. Unfortunately, the Americans didn't think it was workable. Although they had a burns unit on board, they didn't have a paediatrician. Neither did they have any Arabic-speaking staff. It was clear to them that Ali needed a long-term solution. They couldn't take him back to America with them and they weren't prepared to treat him for a few weeks and then dump him back in a slum.'

The failed meeting had left Dr Gorea, who was already exhausted, having worked for several weeks without a break, deeply cynical. 'He thought the Americans weren't interested in helping,' says Peter. 'So when we arrived, he was telling me that the Iraqi people don't need anyone's help.'

Thinking on their feet, Peter and Stewart aired the possibility of getting Ali to Kuwait. 'He said he thought it was viable only if we could organize a helicopter,' says Peter. 'I admitted that I probably couldn't do that, but suggested an ambulance.'

'That boy is not going anywhere in an ambulance,' said Dr Gorea, firmly. 'Eight hours by road would be too painful; it would kill him. He has to go in a helicopter. Only the Americans can help and they are just not interested.'

Peter tried to talk him around. 'I was arguing that an ambulance was better than letting him die upstairs,' he recalls. 'He challenged us to find out if the Kuwaitis would agree before he would talk to us further. To us it didn't seem like such an impossible task.'

Stewart was hopeful that the Kuwaitis would agree to accept Ali. That afternoon he called a friend, Bassima Dalle, who worked at the Canadian embassy in Kuwait. 'She spent the afternoon on the case, ringing government and charity officials in Kuwait to see if they would agree to take Ali,' says Peter, who, meanwhile, had been queuing up in the foyer of the Hotel Palestine at the Civil Affairs desk the Americans had set up there. His intention was to ask the Americans if they would agree to venture into the unsecured and dangerous Sadr City to evacuate Ali to Kuwait.

A scuffle of people swarmed around the hotel lobby: hospital directors trying to get their hospitals fixed, desperate relatives seeking information about their missing loved ones – all of them united by a desire to gain the attention of the gruff American marines behind the counter.

Finally, Peter Wilson was able to talk to Petty Officer Ed Martin himself. 'Ed Martin was also very hostile and fed up with the press. He told me, "I have already wasted time on this case. I don't think we can help." After I proposed Kuwait as a solution, he told me to come back to him if and when we got Kuwaiti agreement.'

The breakthrough came half an hour later back in his room when Peter was able to talk by satellite phone to Abdul Redha Abbas, deputy director of Emergency Services at the Kuwaiti Ministry of Health who had been contacted by Stewart's friend Bassima Dalle. 'The lady from the Canadian Embassy had told me to expect a call from an Australian journalist and a Lebanese man called Innes,' says Abdul Redha Abbas. 'I spoke to them about Ali, and I said we would approach the prime minister of Kuwait about treating him here.' Abdul then talked to the director of his department as well as the Under Secretary for Health, both of whom were already keen to help Ali. 'The Minister of Health then asked the Prime Minister who gave his approval,' recalls Abdul.

Dr Al-Shatti was privy to the discussion in which the Kuwaiti prime minister agreed to help Ali: 'Everyone who heard his terrible story was moved to do what they could to help get Ali out of Baghdad. We feel a responsibility to the Iraqi people and so it was not a difficult decision – after all, we had already helped another eight critical cases – but we needed the Americans to bring him here.' For all their willingness to help, the Kuwaitis were of course powerless to effect Ali's rescue from Sadr City.

Peter returned to the front desk to relay his triumphant news to the marine behind the desk. 'Ed Martin's attitude completely changed when he heard that Ali had been offered treatment in Kuwait,' says Peter. 'He became very friendly, open and collaborative.' It was then that the young American marine uttered the words that were to change Ali's life: 'I may be able to airlift him out of there.'

But before the US Navy Petty Officer could approach his superiors with this idea, he asked Peter to get the hospital to agree to sign the boy over to US troops, and to 'lock in' Ali's family to the plan. 'He pointed out that he couldn't kidnap the kid: he would need a guardian to go with him or some form of legal documentation,' says Peter, who immediately drove with Stewart back to the hospital. The director was happy to agree, as was Ali's family, but no-one had reckoned on the influence of Sheikh Al-Fartousi, the cleric on the doorstep.

'These Shiite religious teachers lost their authority under Saddam, but they got it all back the moment that he was toppled,' explains Mohammed. The Shiites, the majority sect of Islam in Iraq, form more than 60 per cent of its population. They had been suppressed by Saddam, but after he went into hiding they filled the power vacuum, running not only hospitals but also community and cultural centres and police stations. 'Their target was to secure peace, just as our religion demands,' says Mohammed. Unfortunately, Al-Fartousi was suspicious of Stewart and Peter's motives. 'You people have been making these promises for more than a week, but you have done nothing. We are sick of your lies,' he said, in Arabic, to Stewart.

Stewart lost his temper. 'Don't say, "You people" have been doing anything for a week! I don't care what anyone else has said or done – we have told no lies, and we will get Ali out of here as long as you don't ruin things.'

Mohammed was changing Ali's sheets when he received a message to go to the hospital gate where Sheikh Al-Fartousi was in discussion with two journalists. 'I was called down and met Peter Wilson and Stewart Innes from a newspaper called *The Australian*,' says Mohammed. 'They said they had a paper for me to sign to agree for Ali to be treated in Kuwait. They said they were arranging a helicopter to evacuate Ali the following day. I signed the paper, not sure if it would really happen, and told them that I had been chosen by the family to accompany Ali. They said that I should just take what I had with me and that they would equip me with clothes and everything I needed in Kuwait.'

As night fell, Peter and Stewart were able to drive back to the hotel to tell the marine, Ed Martin, that everyone at Al-Sadr Hospital had agreed to the plan. The officer then prepared to tackle his superiors over Ali's case.

The following morning, just as Andrea Catherwood was making her way to Ali's bedside, unaware of the awful tasks she would be asked to help perform, there was a knock on the door of Peter Wilson's room at the Palestine Hotel. Ed Martin introduced Peter to Colonel Kevin Moore, the chief surgeon of the 1st US Marine Division. They then used his satellite phone to call Abdul Redha Abbas, who says, 'They told me that they would fly Ali into their field hospital at our international airport the following day. I said I would be there with an ambulance.'

There were some suggestions in British newspapers that the Pentagon had come under pressure from Downing Street to airlift Ali out of Iraq, but Peter Wilson is adamant that Ali's rescue was a grass-roots operation, organized from the ground up. 'The marines told me that they had heard nothing about Ali Abbas from their superiors,' he insists. 'And they were unaware of any impetus from London. Colonel Moore told me, "They might have got something going in a few days, but this is only happening now because of what you guys have done."'

It is entirely conceivable that political decisions about Ali's future were being taken at a higher level, and certainly the Americans were getting pressure from many sources, not least from the Limbless Association and their contacts. But if the mechanics of the US airlift were finessed by politicians, then this has never been made known publicly. Peter Wilson's reckoning of the detail of Ali's rescue, supported by the testimony of Abdul Redha Abbas at the Ministry of Health in Kuwait, is not only the most plausible account – it appears to be the only account.

If the White House or Downing Street had been directly involved in organizing Ali's evacuation, one might reasonably have expected them to make political capital out of their involvement when the story had a happy ending. On 25 November, at the 2003 Foreign Press Association Media Awards at the Sheraton Park Lane Hotel, London, Peter Wilson had a chance meeting with Tony Blair's former spin-doctor Alastair Campbell, and seized the opportunity to ask him directly about Downing Street's involvement in Ali's story. 'I grabbed a moment with Campbell, the main speaker at the event, and asked him about the Ali story and the suggestion that he had made some calls on Ali's behalf. He said he'd also heard that suggestion and that it was b–s. He said they did not make any calls and had never claimed to have done so. I also asked him whether he'd been involved in asking the Americans to open airspace in order to get Ali out, and he said he'd never heard anything about that.'

But as the Kuwaitis were issuing a press statement confirming that Ali Ismaeel Abbas would be treated in one of their hospitals as soon as he could be airlifted from Iraq, the US Marines were feeling decidedly uneasy about the proposed handover. They knew it was likely to be a twitchy situation: Al-Sadr Hospital was not in coalition control and US troops entering Sadr City, regardless of their humanitarian intention, would therefore be putting themselves at risk. 'The Americans were very concerned about the armed militia,' recalls Stewart Innes. 'Somebody asked whether we could guarantee there would be no guns. I explained that at Al-Sadr Hospital everyone is armed – even the doctors have guns. I mean, who do you speak with to ask to disarm their militia for an hour? How do you approve something like that? Anyway, somehow the agreement sort of filtered through that OK, they will still send a convoy to pick him up.' The plan was to drive Ali to a military base from where he could be flown south to Kuwait and safety.

'All day we thought the helicopter would land,' says Mohammed. 'We waited until 5.30 p.m. and then Andrea had to leave to go back to her hotel.'

At 6 p.m. on Tuesday 15 April 2003, just over half an hour after Andrea Catherwood left the hospital, a US Marines medical evacuation team, led by US lieutenant and doctor Sean Breen, finally arrived at Al-Sadr Hospital to collect the 12-year-old boy. Militiamen guarding the hospital from looters waved in the convoy – two armoured jeeps, a military ambulance and a civilian ambulance.

'I'll never forget the moment that Stewart came into the hospital with the soldiers,' says Mohammed. 'Ali had captured the attention of the media from the early days. I kept hearing promises to get him out, and Stewart, Peter and Andrea stuck to their word. I shall be forever grateful to them for what they each did to help us.'

When it finally came time to hand Ali into the care of the US military, there was little paperwork necessary to formalize the life-saving agreement. There were no medical records on Ali, and no official transfer forms. Instead, a hospital administrator called Khaldoon Khayri took out a blank sheet of paper, scribbled for a while and passed this handwritten 'receipt' for Ali to the other four parties present in the room: Lieutenant Sean Breen, Peter Wilson as the 'mediating agent', Ali's uncle Mohammed, and the Shiite cleric, Sheikh Kathim Al-Fartousi.

Peter Wilson recently managed to get a photocopy of the agreement from the hospital's records – no copy could be made at the time because Al-Sadr's photocopier had broken down. At the top of the paper Khaldoon Khayri has written, 'We are medical evacuation team from America, we receive the patient Ali Abdul Sadda [*sic*], 12 year old, with his uncle to Kuwait. For this reson [*sic*] we sign in presence of Australian press.'

The document is dated 15 April 2003. The hospital director, Dr Gorea, who was absent at the time of Ali's evacuation, has since signed the photocopy.

When Ali was introduced to Lieutenant Breen, a tall American dressed in desert combat fatigues who towered over him, he felt scared. 'I want my uncle! I want my uncle!' he cried out. Mohammed reassured him that he would not be leaving his side, 'There's nothing to worry about, Ali,' he said gently. The military doctor stroked Ali's head and assured him that he would soon be receiving medical care. Then Sheikh Al-Fartousi began to speak. It was a tense moment.

'Before starting war, you should think about all the women

and children who will be injured,' lectured the cleric.

'I'm sorry,' said Lt Sean Breen respectfully. 'I assure you I'm here to help.'

'We are signing this paper and giving you this boy hoping to get him back and that you will take care of him. There must be no cheating or playing games,' the cleric boomed.

'We agree to take Ali into our care, and into our hearts,' responded the doctor quietly.

A few minutes later, the cleric asked Innes to privately 'tell the lieutenant that we realize the bombing was probably a mistake as you were probably aiming at Ba'ath Party targets and we hope there will be more of this sort of cooperation'.

Soon the stretcher, conveying Ali's makeshift metal cage covered with a pink blanket, was rolled through the hospital corridor towards a bloodstained lift. Ali, bewildered by what would happen next, was afraid to leave his doting nurse, Fatin Sharhad and he cried out for her.

As the stretcher was being wheeled into the lift, Sheikh Al-Fartousi confided in Mohammed. 'He said to me, "I don't trust these Americans. What will they do with the boy?" And for that reason he had arranged a cameraman to film what was happening with a video camera,' Mohammed recalls.

In the lift Ali excitedly asked the cameraman recording the scene to show him his picture. 'One minute he was the victim of a horrible injury, the next he's an excited child,' says Peter Wilson. 'Kids of that age are already flicking between childhood and adulthood, but it was kind of extraordinary.'

Ali winced a few times as he was wheeled over bumps in the corridor. They irritated the second-degree burns that surrounded the deeper wounds on his pelvis and shoulder. But he also felt excited about finally getting proper treatment, and pain relief. His head was full of images: eating with his hands, playing football and washing his face.

Mohammed says that a US armoured military ambulance was

originally designated to transport Ali to the airport, but that Sheikh Al-Fartousi refused to allow this. 'He explained that it was not appropriate and that he should go by hospital ambulance instead,' he says.

Stewart recalls the cleric's words: 'He said, "No, no, we have our own vehicles. We can transport our own people. We don't need Western assistance," and started off on this whole monologue thing. So they put him in one of their ambulances – and it doesn't have a wheel. They put him in another, and they don't have a key for it, so they pull him out. He went through three ambulances before they got a combination of an ambulance that works, has four wheels, a driver and a set of keys. It was chaos.'

The situation was made all the more chaotic by the large crowd that had gathered outside the hospital in the half-light of dusk. It was a tense situation for all concerned, but it was one that Sheikh Al-Fartousi was determined to milk. 'He asked me whether they could just say a little prayer "as is our tradition",' says Stewart. 'I thought it was going to be a silent prayer, but then the *imam* shouts a verse, punches the air, and the whole place was in uproar as three hundred people responded. The marines must have thought this was it: there's a revolution right here in front of them. If a car had backfired at that moment, there would have been a bloodbath.'

Peter recalls this impromptu rally of chanting as the ambulance emerged on to the street outside the hospital. He believes the Iraqis punching the air were celebrating, as clerics walked ahead of the military convoy leading chants of 'Allah is Great!' and 'May Allah bless the child!' But Mohammed says that not all Iraqis welcomed Ali's removal. 'There were young men there that day who felt angry and helpless. They wanted to know what the Americans were doing there.' When these proud, angry and humiliated men discovered that the Americans were helping one of their own, Mohammed says that their sense of frustration increased: the people who had hurt them in an attempt to bring them liberation were now helping those they had unwittingly injured. 'I prayed that Allah would deliver us to safety,' recalls Mohammed.

Ali's procession could proceed no faster than walking pace. The large, chanting crowd pressed in on the vehicles as they crawled through the sprawling slum. Young boys jumped on the rear bumpers to peer inside as the crowd surged forward. 'Sheikh Al-Fartousi was hamming it up,' says Peter. 'He was walking in front of the convoy ambulance holding hands with Mohammed, then they released two pigeons into the mêlée and embraced. When the cleric saw Stewart get out of our vehicle at the back of the convoy, he went to take his hand as well. He was then walking with Mohammed on one side and Stewart on the other. It was a big, theatrical gesture.'

The marines in the military ambulance and two jeeps escorting the hospital ambulance were relieved when, finally, the crowd started to thin. As Mohammed stepped into Ali's ambulance, Sheikh Al-Fartousi kissed him on top of his head and gave him an extravagant embrace. The convoy then picked up speed on the 10-kilometre journey east to Baladiyat, the headquarters of Saddam's secret police where Mayada Al-Askari had been imprisoned and tortured four years earlier, and that had now been appropriated as a base by the 7th US Marines. While Peter Wilson waited at this 'secured fortress' for clearance to enter, Ali was taken from his ambulance to a tented hospital in the grounds, a MASH-style set up, where he was treated for 20 minutes. 'This is the right time to get him out,' said nurse Lieutenant Aaron Jacobs. 'He needs to get to a major burns facility fast.' Within minutes Ali's stretcher was being carried by six soldiers towards a waiting Black Hawk Medevac helicopter.

He whimpered with pain as his stretcher was slid inside. Charred and weeping burns covered almost all the front of his torso and stretched to his legs and part of his back. The military doctors shared the fears of the Iraqi medics that without urgent treatment, blood infections would soon kill him. 'Ali was screaming for water,' says Peter Wilson. 'But the nurse explained that he was hot because his body thermostat wasn't working properly, and assured him that he'd feel much cooler with the flow of air in the helicopter.'

And yet, through the fog of his pain and discomfort, Ali felt strangely excited about the adventure. He says he'd always wanted to travel, though he'd never imagined it would be like this.

As Mohammed stepped up into the aircraft with its crew of four, Stewart and Peter promised him that they would soon see him in Kuwait. 'He was understandably nervous because of the history of bad blood between Kuwait and Iraq, so we said we would join him there and help get him organized,' says Peter. Mohammed concurs, 'I was very worried about Ali's wounds, but I was also concerned about what sort of reception we would receive in Kuwait. My country had looted Kuwait, our soldiers did harm, yet still the Kuwaitis rushed to help us as soon as Saddam's regime ended. I didn't know what the Kuwaitis would think of us, or how they would treat us, because of the history of the invasion. It would have been reasonable for them to dislike us.'

The helicopter hovered for a moment before lifting noisily into the sky and turning south-east towards the Imam Ali US airbase in Nasiriya, two and a half hours' flying time away, and en route to Kuwait. It wasn't considered a particularly risky flight. No-one was targeting helicopters back then, and US helicopters were making countless routine flights between Nasiriya and the recently liberated Baghdad – one reason why Wilson thinks it was relatively straightforward for the local troops on the ground to effect Ali's mercy flight without recourse to higher powers, though some disagree with him.

As the helicopter flew Ali further from home than he had ever been, Mohammed was nursing grave concerns behind the façade of happiness and hope he had been wearing for days. 'When we got into the helicopter and left Baghdad, I very much doubted that Ali would live. He was in a bad state. His wounds had suppurated and there was a bad smell,' he recalls. 'I was hoping inside myself that he would die, not because he had lost his parents or his arms but because the pain was unbearable: all his body was burned. As the helicopter took off, I honestly expected that I would be returning from Kuwait in two days' time with his body.'

At 9.30 p.m. the helicopter descended from the jet-black sky and on to an airstrip at the Imam Ali airbase in southern Iraq. A team of doctors were waiting. 'One US soldier there was deeply touched by Ali,' says Mohammed. 'He let him watch a Tom and Jerry cartoon on a compact DVD player and TV while he lay on a stretcher.' For a few minutes Ali was able to forget his pain. The vulnerable human cargo was then transferred to a US Marine Corps C130 transport plane for the onward journey to the American field hospital at Kuwait International Airport.

As Ali was carried into the distinctive snub-nosed plane on the evening of Tuesday 15 April, the telephone at Diana Morgan's home in London began to ring. 'It was a media contact, phoning to tell us that Ali had just been rescued from the hospital and was now going to be treated in Kuwait. This was the most fantastic news,' says Diana who now believed that Ali had a good chance of survival, and of receiving the sort of care that would one day return his independence just as hers had been returned 13 years earlier.

But at 2.00 a.m. on Wednesday morning, as the plane touched down at the American field hospital on the fringes of Kuwait International Airport, Ali's chances of survival were still estimated at only one in two.

PART TWO

Kuwait

CHAPTER ELEVEN

'I Was Eager to See a New Country'

'I was excited about going in the helicopter because it was my first ever flight. It was very noisy. There were two American doctors on board and two captains, I think. I was very afraid – I thought we might fall out of the sky at any time. We left Baghdad at 7 p.m. and flew to Nasiriya. Then we went by cargo plane to Kuwait. We arrived early in the morning and I didn't sleep at all. Once we got to Kuwait, they put drips in my feet; and then as soon as I arrived at the hospital, I had a skin-graft operation.

'As I left Iraq I was very, very much in pain about what had happened to my family, but I was also very excited to be going to a new place for the first time. I had never travelled before and I was eager to see a new country.'

Ali Ismaeel Abbas

The affluent metropolis of Kuwait City, with its flashy high-rise glass and steel skyline, did not feel like a city less than 160 kilometres from a war-zone. The sprawling tented American military camp fuelling the supply lines into Iraq lay just a few kilometres to the north of the city, but for most Kuwaitis life continued as normal, underscored with the relief that came from knowing that, after 24 years, Saddam Hussein's neighbouring regime had at last been toppled. The prosperous citizens of

Kuwait City drove their large, glamorous cars into traffic jams along the palm-lined highways, filled the Western-style shopping malls with their designer labels, and floated their jet skis and windsurfers across the warm waters of the Persian Gulf, along 200 kilometres of sun-drenched coastline baking beneath the searing Middle Eastern sun.

Kuwait may be just a twentieth the size of its hulking northern neighbour, and one of the world's smallest countries, but its oil-based economy means it is also one of the richest. Slightly larger than Wales, it boasts almost one-tenth of the world's known reserves of this liquid, black gold. Yet before the discovery of oil in 1938, 11 years after it was first struck in Iraq, Kuwait was a desert wilderness. Before the construction of desalination plants, every drop of fresh water had to be imported by tanker – from Iraq. It took just 50 years for the oil industry to transform Kuwait into a prosperous welfare state under the feudal embrace of its ruling family. There is no income tax, petrol costs 10p a litre, and education and healthcare is freely available to all.

Before the Iraqi invasion of 1990, Kuwait and Iraq shared their border peacefully. There was a long history of inter-marriage between the nations. However, as Iraq became increasingly impoverished under Saddam's rule and the borders effectively closed, rumours of Kuwait's increasing prosperity filtered through to Iraqi citizens, many of whom, like Mohammed, said that they couldn't help feeling envious.

The most covetous Iraqi of all was Saddam Hussein. Kuwait may have gained independence from Britain in 1961, after more than two hundred years of protection dating from the time of the Ottoman Empire, but he chose not to recognize Kuwait's nationhood. In August 1990 his murderous troops arrived and he boasted to the world that he had annexed his affluent, oil-rich neighbour as Iraq's rightful nineteenth province. During the war with Iran Saddam had promised to mobilize his troops to protect Kuwait if it were to be attacked. Now his own forces set about trashing the country, and killing and torturing hundreds of Kuwaitis. Six hundred oil wells were torched, the Persian Gulf was flooded with oil, luxury hotels were sacked, and shops and warehouses were plundered.

Then in February 1991 US forces, helped by troops from many of the world's nations, liberated the emirate from the tyrant and won Kuwait's loyalty forever.

When the evacuated Iraqi children started to arrive in Kuwait for treatment, some Kuwaitis felt uneasy about caring for the offspring of their former oppressors. They couldn't help but associate them with their memories of Saddam's army. The invasion of their peace-loving country by the neighbouring regime 13 years earlier had left a legacy of bitterness. Saddam might have gone, but behind Kuwait's sheen of prosperity the scars of the Iraqi occupation were still raw. Some six hundred Kuwaitis seized by Saddam's soldiers still remained unaccounted for, and the Kuwaiti people had lived in permanent fear of another Iraqi invasion. The financial and emotional cost of raising Kuwait from the ashes had been enormous.

'People had deep wounds following the Iraqi invasion,' asserts Dr Ahmad Al-Shatti, the director of Health Education and the Media Department at Kuwait's Ministry of Health. 'Many people still felt bitter, and they included some of our medical personnel. One physiotherapist told me that she would never have dreamed of shaking hands with any Iraqi in her life, let alone treating or helping one. The same lady colleague just forgot all this the minute she saw the children in pain and tears.'

As the highly professional team at Ibn Sina Hospital began to work with the frightened and injured innocents, those harbouring prejudices soon found that their own wounds were also beginning to heal.

*   *   *

In the early hours of 16 April 'Patient 103' arrived at a smart Kuwaiti hospital ringed by ornamental palm trees. He was immediately pitched into a chaotic media scrum. Nearly 60 journalists had gathered to report on the fragile young boy who had already become Ibn Sina Hospital's most famous patient. Although Ali was the ninth critically ill Iraqi child to be airlifted to Kuwait, this scared-looking boy had already become the Kuwaiti Ministry of Health's biggest ever news-story.

Ali's ambulance arrived outside the sparkling white hospital a little before 4 a.m. His stretcher was pulled out by a turbaned orderly as Ali peered with frightened eyes around the rim of the metal cage that had protected him for the past 17 days. He was dazzled by the camera lights, and overwhelmed by a bewildering mêlée of strangers surging forward to peer at him. Here, at his most vulnerable moment, the attention of the whole world was focused upon him.

Abdul Redha Abbas, the distinguished-looking deputy director of Emergency Services, who had helped organize Ali's evacuation from Iraq with Peter Wilson and Colonel Moore, had met Ali at the airport and accompanied him by ambulance to Ibn Sina Hospital. 'Ali was really tired and weak when he arrived in Kuwait,' says Abdul, who was responsible for establishing Kuwait's first paramedic facility in 1977. 'He told me, "Please, no noise," but when we arrived at the hospital the scene there was bedlam.' Now he attempted to clear a path through the tumult of whirring and clicking cameras. 'The patient is tired! The patient is tired!' Abdul shouted, as he waved a clipboard at the swarm of journalists. 'I don't need this hustle.'

Even with his uncle by his side, Ali was frightened by the unfamiliar surroundings and the maelstrom breaking all around him as he was wheeled into his third hospital in as many weeks. Journalists crowded around him in the narrow corridor. Ali bit his lip and cried out to his uncle who bent over to reassure him. 'There was a great surge of TV crews trying to film Ali,' says

Alexandra Williams, a news reporter for the *Daily Mirror* who had been waiting outside the hospital for 24 hours since her newsdesk had heard that Ali was about to be airlifted to Kuwait. Arguments were breaking out between the journalists as several agency reporters pushed into intensive care. 'There were massive stand-up rows between journalists,' says Alexandra. 'We couldn't believe that they were going into a sterile area when this little boy was in absolute agony. He'd had everything taken from him. All he had left was his dignity and now even that was under threat.'

The plastic surgeons who awaited Ali's arrival at Ibn Sina Hospital's Al-Babtain Centre for Burns and Plastic Surgery, the second biggest centre for skin grafts in Europe and the Middle East, knew that the small boy who had been evacuated to their sterile sanctuary would be seriously ill and in urgent need of specialized burns treatment. They were shocked, however, not by the extent of his burns, but by their deteriorated condition.

'On arrival he was in very bad shape – he was not stable. He was anaemic, dehydrated and in shock. His burns were badly infected. The infection had by now eaten into the remaining tissue meaning that they were all now third-degree, full skin thickness burns,' explains Dr Imad Al-Najada, the 40-year-old senior registrar on call that night who had himself been threatened with execution by an Iraqi soldier during the first Gulf War. 'All the layers of skin and fat down to the flesh had gone on 35 per cent of his body area. His trauma was con-siderable. There is a high incidence of mortality from this type of wound infection. Without surgery I doubt he would have survived.'

Dr Al-Najada's clinical recollection is measured and objective, but Mohammed reveals that when the surgeon first saw Ali's burns he confided in him as a fellow Shiite Muslim that 'his heart sort of stopped'. 'The doctor said he asked himself how he would treat this boy, and said he had prayed for guidance,' says Mohammed. 'He said he thought only a miracle could help him. But he also said that he thought that there would be a miracle.'

Dr Al-Najada and his colleague Dr Nabil knew they had to act quickly. Their young patient was feverish, and they could tell, even before clinically examining him, that his body was in the early stages of septic shock. 'There was bacteria in his blood and he was lucky not to have suffered multi-organ failure,' says Dr Al-Najada, who gave Ali a blood transfusion and began to rehydrate him with a litre of saline solution in readiness for surgery.

Outside the journalists could hear Ali crying out as he was examined. 'His screams in intensive care were the most distressing thing I've ever heard,' says Alexandra Williams. Later, she was to write, 'It was disbelief, trauma, sheer hell. I sobbed in the hospital car park that night.'

Within a few hours the consultant in charge of the plastic surgery centre had arrived to review Ali's case. Dr Ibrahim el-Sayed Ghoneim, an avuncular Egyptian who had trained as a plastic surgeon in Glasgow, scrubbed up and joined Dr Al-Najada in theatre for the delicate, life-saving surgery that Ali should have had within hours of the missile strike.

In skin-graft surgery the groundwork is all-important. You can only harvest so much skin from a patient's body, and only from those areas unaffected by burns. And before you do so you must be absolutely certain that the grafted skin will adhere completely to the underlying tissue, not curl away and die. The first step towards creating the optimum conditions for a skin graft following severe burning is to remove every millimetre of inflamed, infected or dead tissue from the burn site. It took the plastic surgeons 90 minutes to cut away the burned and infected tissue, revealing the healthy, bright pink tissue beneath, which was then covered with a temporary graft from the hospital's skin bank. This would help keep the burns clean in preparation for the skin graft proper a few days later. During the first operation the medical team also tidied up Ali's amputations, suturing his residual right arm and affixing a skin graft over the left.

'Ali's burns were so severe that he had only a small amount of unburned skin, on his back and thighs, suitable for skin-graft surgery,' explains Dr Al-Najada. 'That's why we didn't want to rush anything. Before doing the permanent skin grafts, we had to be certain that the raw area is clean and not bleeding.'

Dr Al-Najada told Ali's uncle that he now had no doubts whatsoever about Ali's chances of survival. And after surgery Ali even felt well enough to answer a few questions from journalists wearing gowns and face masks. One Egyptian journalist asked Ali what he would like as a gift. 'I would very much like a small television with cartoons inside it please,' said Ali, mindful of the amazing gadget he'd seen in Nasiriya. When another journalist asked him, more philosophically, what he was thinking about, he replied that he hoped no other child would have to suffer as he had suffered. Then he thanked her for her interest. It was clear that he hadn't lost his magical touch with the media.

That night, for the first time since he was injured, Ali found himself lying on clean sheets in a sterile environment, surrounded by beeping machines. The facilities were in stark contrast to the chaos of the front-line hospitals he'd left behind in Baghdad: there were no men with guns guarding this hospital or attempting to loot its contents, no fraught doctors crying at the pain they had to inflict on their patients without anaesthetic, no bloodstained lifts, or swarms of flies crawling over his body. With his uncle Mohammed staying in a private room next door, Ibn Sina Hospital felt reassuringly safe. And, for the first time in 16 days, Ali Abbas was no longer in pain.

Some of Mohammed's fears had also been laid to rest. 'Fortunately, I soon discovered that these were lovely people who really cared about Ali. We thought Kuwait hated us. It seemed strange to be getting treatment from "the enemy", but no-one seemed to carry any grudges. In fact, we were over-whelmed by people's kindness.'

As Mohammed had climbed into the helicopter in Baghdad, nursing his private fears, Peter Wilson and Stewart Innes had promised him that they would soon join him in Kuwait City. After returning to the Palestine Hotel for a drink with Ed Martin, the US Navy Petty Officer, who had helped arrange Ali's transfer, the journalists packed their bags in preparation for their drive south the following morning in their now battered four-wheel-drive. They started off in convoy with a group of CNN vehicles, but were soon caught up in a terrific sandstorm that swept across their path as they battled down the eastern highway on the edge of the Iraqi desert towards the sanctuary of the Kuwaiti border. 'It was fairly hairy,' says Peter Wilson. 'These were rough roads and it was impossible to see.' Just before they left Iraq they stopped to refuel the vehicle from metal jerrycans on the roof of the four-wheel-drive. 'A gang of kids immediately gathered and became increasingly aggressive,' says Peter. 'Suddenly they ripped open the back doors of the vehicle and started grabbing our boxes and bags of food. At that moment a truck on the other side of the road screamed to a halt. Two Iraqi men jumped out and pursued the boys.' In disbelief, Peter realized that the truck driver and his companion were after the boxes and bags for themselves. 'It was a completely sponta-neous crime. I couldn't believe what I was seeing.'

Accepting that they would have to ditch their stolen belongings, Stewart prepared to pull back on to the highway. Suddenly, with a jolt of despair, Peter realized that one of the boxes the boys had pulled out contained the only remaining photographs of Ali's family. Before the reporter had left Baghdad, a *Daily Mirror* journalist had given him a small plastic bag and had asked if the Australian could pass the pictures it contained on to Mohammed.

'We swerved off the highway and on to a dirt track, down which the boys had run,' says Peter. 'We caught them several hundred metres further on, over a crest, going through the loot that they'd managed to hold on to. They were shocked to see us coming and immediately scattered.'

Peter saw one of the fleeing youths jettison a small plastic package. 'The family snaps!' says Peter, triumphantly. He grabbed the package from the dust and ran back to the car.

Eight hours after they had left Baghdad the weary men finally arrived in Kuwait City, just as Ali was settling down to his first night of real sleep. They went up to the hospital the next day, and found Ali's strength much improved. He had managed to eat some breakfast and lunch, and his fever had subsided.

'We helped Mohammed deal with the press, who were being fairly feral, and then we took Mohammed to buy clothes,' says Peter. It was becoming clear that Ali's uncle would be staying in Kuwait for some time, yet he had brought nothing with him other than the prayer equipment he'd been using at Al-Sadr while he was staying with Ali: a prayer mat, a tablet of ceremonial earth which, as a Shiite Muslim he touched with his forehead as he prayed, and a rosary. As he wandered around a smart shopping precinct, Mohammed struggled to believe what he was seeing. 'I'd always heard people say that Kuwait was wealthy, but I hadn't expected it to also feel so safe – people didn't even lock their cars. But I also felt sad to see this beautiful modern country. Why, when Iraq has so many rich resources, are we suffering so much? Saddam has a lot to answer for. He has destroyed everything. Iraq modernized before Kuwait, but these days the contrast couldn't be greater.'

Earlier that day Ali had been visited by Kuwait's deputy prime minister and foreign minister, Sheikh Sabah Al-Ahmad Al-Sabah (now prime minister). 'He has visited all the children so far brought from Iraq, and has given orders to trace their families and bring them over to see the kids,' Dr Al-Shatti told

Mohammed. Sheikh Sabah had made no secret of his eagerness to improve relations with other Arab nations following recent events.

To Ali's delight the Egyptian journalist also returned with the compact DVD player Ali had asked for, along with ten cartoon discs. Somebody else bought him a small television. 'What really surprised me was the way the Kuwaitis "opened the doors of their houses to us", as we say,' says Mohammed. 'We were visited all day long by people who wanted to know how Ali was doing, and this was to continue day after day. They offered us support and brought presents, some of which Ali sent to the other children in the hospital. Meeting Sheikh Sabah lifted our spirits still further. I had soon changed my views about the Kuwaitis 100 per cent.'

The day after he arrived in Kuwait, in an attempt to assess the psychological impact of his ordeal Ali was examined by a psychiatrist for the first time since being hospitalized. 'It was clear that Ali had been suffering from post-traumatic stress disorder when he was in Iraq,' explains Dr Al-Najada, who says Ali demonstrated two key factors of the syndrome: depression and loss of appetite. 'But Ali had made a good recovery early on because of the support he had received from his family, friends and the media. The psychiatrist prescribed him some drugs, but we decided not to give them to him as he was doing fine without them.'

Dr Al-Najada himself was immediately impressed with Ali's attitude. 'It is not just a matter of being physically strong,' he told journalists at Ali's bedside. 'He's a very clever child and he is just so, so determined. Today he noticed improvements made in his condition since yesterday.'

The doctor anticipated that the boy would need a week to ten days of initial treatment in the burns centre before he would be ready to receive the first of two major skin-graft operations. These would be followed by several months of rehabilitation,

Ali's mother: Azhar Ali Dhahir, wearing her traditional *hijab* (religious headscarf).

Ali's father: Ismaeel Abbas Hamza, photographed in 1983.

A happy family: (*from right to left*) Ali's mother Azhar, Ali, his sister Lamya'a (*centre*), his younger brother Abbas and his sister Isma'a.

Three brothers: Ali with his younger brothers, Abbas (*right*) and Hamza (*left*).

Ali's step-mother Layla, Mohammed's sister.

Stewart Innes (*left*) helped effect Ali's rescue from Sadr City. He is surrounded here by members of Ali's family including Ali's adored little sister Hadeel (*front*).

Ali's uncle Kareem stands in the ruin of Ali's house in the Arab Al-Khrsa, southern Baghdad.

We are medical evacuate team from America, we receive the patient ALI Abdul Sadfa 12 year old, with his uncle to Kuwait for this reson we sign in presence of Australian press

BREEDLOVE
MO LT M. USNR
1ST FSSG 4th MAR,

PETER WILSON
"THE AUST RALIAN"

15/4/2005 Thuesday
ح ٥٠٨ ١٥/١٠ الثلاثاء

بواقع ذلك مفاده وبين المرضى
على ١.٢٠ عبدالله ١١ سنة مع عمه
دنى ١ الكوين. ٦. بوقيع نسبت

محمد عبد العزز ١ - عينى
صليقه اعذري زنون عنتى

M. GOREA
DR. MOUAFAK GOREA
CONSULTANT SURGEON

The scrap of paper that became a 'receipt' for Ali, signed at Al-Sadr Hospital, Baghdad, before he was released into American care en-route to Kuwait City.

Relief: Ali finds comfort in Ibn Sina Hospital, Kuwait City.

A devoted nursing team: Mohammed (*left*), Ali and the nursing staff at Al-Babtain burns unit at Ibn Sina Hospital, Kuwait.

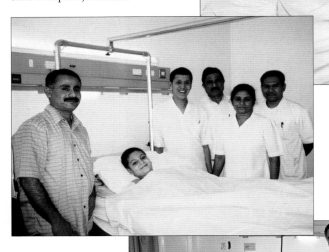

A private room at Ibn Sina hospital: (*right to left*) Dr Imad Al-Najada, uncle Mohammed, Ahmed (in wheel-chair), Ali and Rasoul, another Iraqi patient being treated at Al-Babtain Centre for Burns and Plastic Surgery.

Above: Nafisah encourages Ali to paint with his right foot to produce his first painting.

Below: Ali's first painting with his foot, reproduced on cards sold to raise money for Ali by the British Ladies of Kuwait.

The Kuwaiti Prime Minister, Sheikh Sabah Al-Ahmad Al-Sabah, and Ali at the press conference just before Ali and Ahmed's departure to the UK.

Ali and Ahmed answer questions from the media with the Kuwaiti Minister of Health, Mohammed Al-Jarralleh.

Ali leaving Kuwait in Sheikh Sabah's private jet on 7 August 2003.

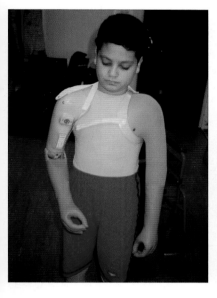

Left: Ali tries out his new arms for the first time, in mid-October 2003.

Below: Ali with Penny Buttonshaw, senior physiotherapist at Queen Mary's Hospital, Roehampton.

Ali's new extended family in London: (*left to right*) Zafar Khan, Dr Al-Shatti, Diana Morgan, Lara Morgan, Ahmed (in wheelchair), Ali, uncle Mohammed, Mr Mohammed Hamza.

My hero: Ali and Ahmed meet David Beckham and members of the England football team.

Ali returns to Baghdad in December 2003 and demonstrates how he can eat an orange with his new arms, watched by (*left to right*) Mohammed's children, Luoi and Marwa, and Ali's sisters Hana'a, Shahla'a and Lamya'a.

An important friend: (*left to right*) uncle Mohammed, Ali, Ahmed and his father are honoured to meet Kuwaiti Prime Minister Sheikh Sabah again.

after which he would be able to be fitted with artificial arms.

Ali might have been in Kuwait for only 36 hours, but already the hospital was fielding calls from around the world, from individuals and organizations offering to make donations towards prosthetic limbs to replace those he had lost. He was gaining in strength and now there was hope for his future. Dr Al-Shatti was tasked with coordinating these offers, as well as accommodating the world's media with their insatiable appetite for news about Ali. 'Usually the doctors treating a famous patient here are required to make one or two brief statements: we had this huge story unfolding and a constant stream of journalists asking questions. We had never been through something like this before. I had to try to balance the needs of the media with the privacy of the patient,' explains Dr Al-Shatti, who understood why Ali was the subject of such international attention. 'Ali's story is uniquely moving – not just his burns and the loss of his parents, but the fact Ali was a successful boy who was well dressed, liked his work and was always cheerful. It is these bits of information that build up the sense of a real tragedy.'

Ali's room had now been declared a sterile area. Journalists who wanted to interview him had to conduct interviews by telephone from the other side of a large window while Mohammed sat patiently by his bedside. Mohammed speaks only a few words of English, so one of the doctors would normally translate reporters' questions. The *Daily Mirror*'s Alexandra Williams was one who visited every day for two and a half weeks. 'I used a lot of sign language through the glass to try and cheer Ali up,' she says. 'He was sedated and looked completely bewildered in these alien surroundings. He was subdued and homesick, didn't really know where he was and wasn't allowed to see any other children, but he still always managed to be really polite and obliging.'

Ali was also interviewed by Stephanie Condron of the *Metro*, the free London newspaper that had first told the world his story. 'He told me that he was worried what his school friends would think when they saw him, and begged me to get him some new arms,' she says.

Many members of the public started to send Ali gifts and get-well cards. 'After Ali had been in Kuwait about a week, soft toys and sports gear began to arrive from around the world,' says Mohammed. Soon there were so many colourful music players, radios and sets of head-phones that Mohammed was able to send a full box of them back home.

Ali was also given a football-shaped radio alarm clock, a gigantic teddy bear and a fluffy black-and-white toy dog. One cherished parcel from the UK was packed with Manchester United football memorabilia. It came from Thomas Edwards, a garrulous 50-year-old Mancunian who drives a burger van in Salford and is an ardent fan of the club. In the days after Ali's photograph was first published he was one of several thousand members of the public who telephoned the Limbless Association to make a donation to Ali's Fund. 'I've always considered myself a bit of a tough guy, but when I saw the image of Ali, well, something hit me like a ton of bricks. I'd got sight of the TV pictures as I turned back to say ta-ra to my daughter, Emma. Ali looked so much like my four-year-old grandson. Boy, did I cry. I kept hearing that he would die if he wasn't rescued. I was talking about Ali so much that half my customers deserted me and started going to McDonald's, but I had to spread the word.'

While Ali was still in Baghdad, Thomas made 43 inter-national calls to the White House, the Pentagon and the American 24-hour news station CNN. He also phoned the Limbless Association and offered to go to Baghdad to drive Ali out himself. 'When I heard he'd been evacuated to Kuwait, I cried with relief all the way home,' he says. 'Somehow, Ali had changed my life.' Thomas began calling Ibn Sina Hospital on a daily basis and was soon receiving regular reports on Ali's progress from Abner Mayol, one of Ali's favourite nurses.

Thomas and his wife, Jackie, went on a huge spending spree for Ali. They sent him Marks and Spencer's T-shirts, shorts, underpants, pyjamas, socks, and so many items of Nike sportswear that Mohammed assumed he must work for the sportswear company. When coaxed to reveal how much he spent, Mr Edwards says, 'Well, with the postage, we didn't get much change out of £600.

'My family are all travelling showmen, fairground folk, and they delved into their pockets,' says Thomas, who even planned to travel out to Kuwait at one point. 'My son didn't get it: he thought I must have a bird in Ibiza, but I couldn't explain, even to myself, why Ali had made such an impression on me.'

Ali had also made an impact on a French missionary and film-maker, Catherine Ecolivet, who has spent years in developing countries. 'I have been exposed to many – too many – heart-breaking faces,' she says. 'My principle has always been not to get involved with just one child: I dealt with the hopeless feeling of injustice trying to deliver a great project instead.' But on a quiet, spring evening in Paris she was getting ready to leave for Cannes to promote her latest film about human rights when she saw Ali on the news. 'With his baby cheeks, curly hair and striking eyes, I saw the face of a wounded angel. To say I was overwhelmed would be an understatement: his tragedy hit me fully in the soul. Forget the long-held principle of not being involved with only one child. It was no longer an issue.'

The television newscaster was announcing Ali's evacuation to Kuwait. 'I'd never been there,' says Catherine. 'I didn't know one Kuwaiti citizen, but I had the feeling of being electrified.' After a sleepless night, she sent Ali a fax, saying she hoped to come to Kuwait, to 'talk about your dreams'.

Within two weeks Catherine's visa had arrived and she met Ali for the first time. 'He was lying on his bed, covered with a white sheet going to his neck. The curly hair had been cut and the baby cheeks had disappeared as well. But the striking eyes and soft voice were there. I had taken him a stethoscope as a gift. Ali smiled when he heard my heartbeat. I told him that he could hear my heart, but he was also in my heart and would stay there forever.' Despite being a Catholic, Catherine also took several Korans to his bedside: a large one to keep at home, and a smaller one in a wooden box to travel with. 'Ali kissed the new Korans; then Mohammed put the big one on the table and the small one in the box by his bedside.'

The afternoon she arrived – Catherine was to stay in Kuwait for the next month – she took photographs of Ali; then asked him to select his favourite. The next day she returned with the framed print, a picture of Ali and Mohammed smiling together, and placed it by his bedside. She also took photographs of every staff member and, in due course, all Ali's new friends. 'We began to build an album of his new extended family. I told Ali that even if his dreams have to be reshaped, that he shouldn't give up on them.'

CHAPTER TWELVE

'It Looks Just Like a Real Arm'

'I was fazed when I first arrived in Kuwait: it's the first country I have been to outside of Iraq. I was telling myself, "This is good for me. Iraq has a big shortage of treatment and medicine, and now I'm going to a country where they have good treatment and medicine." I tried to reassure myself it was going to be better. When I arrived in Kuwait, there was medication and sedatives, and I was happy and relieved. It made a big difference. I felt very much safer because they had clean bandages, they had medication, and they really treated me well.'

Ali Ismaeel Abbas

The Al-Babtain Centre for Burns and Plastic Surgery has an international reputation. The unit is at the forefront of plastic surgery research, and offers specialities including tumour removal and cosmetic operations. Both Dr Ibrahim and Dr Al-Najada specialize in reconstructive surgery. When a child comes in requiring an operation for a cleft palate or hare lip, for example, the consultant and his senior registrar will always carry out this delicate procedure with particular care, in a bid to help the children integrate fully into society with minimum scarring. Dr Al-Najada's son Abdullah is the same age as Ali;

both Dr Al-Najada and his superior appreciated the social challenges Ali would face in the future.

Ali had been told that over the course of the next two weeks he would undergo several operations until eventually there would be a seamless join between the burns and the rest of his skin. But first a surprise was in store. In Baghdad he had confided a love of football to Andrea Catherwood, the ITN journalist, and on 23 April David Beckham and his Manchester United team dedicated their vital Champions league clash with Real Madrid to Ali. They won 4–3 at Old Trafford, but were still knocked out of the contest. Beckham said the squad had been touched by Ali's plight and he had signed a shirt for him: 'To Ali, God bless, love David Beckham.' This was the most exciting gift Ali had received. He began to dream of playing for the team himself.

As the days passed, there was a growing affection between Ali and his uncle Mohammed. After the first operation to clean his wounds, Ali contracted the MRSA bug and skin-graft surgery was delayed by a week. No-one other than the core medical staff and his uncle Mohammed were permitted to enter his room. 'I stayed from 6 a.m. to 11 p.m. every single day, for days and days,' he says with a mock-weary smile. 'The only time I left was when I had lunch or prayed: Ali didn't let me out of his sight, and it could get a bit exhausting. I felt like his personal assistant, and there were a lot of instructions: "Change the cartoon, answer the phone, speak to the journalists looking in at me through the window, turn the light on, turn the light off." Then at night, once I'd got him settled and he seemed to be sleeping, I would creep towards the door – and the cry would come "Where are you going?" and I'd be called back to attend to some new request.' By looking after Ali, Mohammed was honouring his friendship to Ismaeel and fulfilling his familial duty, but his relationship with Ali was genuinely deepening. Ali ate reluctantly at first, but he tenderly fed him grapes, biscuits or forkfuls of rice and stew.

On 27 April, 11 days after the first operation, Dr Ghoneim judged that Ali was finally ready to receive the first part of the two-stage permanent skin-graft operation. Ali had reached a milestone on his road to recovery, but, as he had a relatively small donor area of unburned skin, a 100 per cent first-time take-up of the grafted skin was imperative. There could be no second chances.

His uncle kissed his forehead. Then, once under general anaesthetic, the temporary skin graft was removed, before a thin layer of skin no more than 0.3 millimetres thick, was harvested from Ali's back and thighs with a specialized skin-graft knife. Each delicate sheet of living skin was then passed through a machine that punctured it with thousands of tiny holes, allowing each small piece to be stretched out wide enough to cover the large burns on Ali's chest, back and upper abdomen. Small, temporary metal staples were used to fix each graft in position. Mohammed paced nervously during the four-hour operation – he says it felt like eight hours.

'When I woke up from the skin-graft operation, it was painful,' remembers Ali. 'But I was focusing on the future, on having arms, on the forthcoming treatment. I was always thinking, "They'll treat me. They'll make me better."'

And he was right. The operation had been more successful than the doctors had expected. 'It was very good and fast,' says Dr Ghoneim. His team had hoped to cover 50 per cent of Ali's burns with the permanent skin grafts during the operation, but were able to cover 80 per cent. They also replaced the temporary skin graft on his remaining burns in readiness for the final skin-graft operation a week later. 'The surgeons have told me that they are very happy,' said Dr Ahmad Al-Shatti in a brief press conference. 'The kid is smiling and responding well. He's doing just fine.'

The next day Ali's dressings were removed, a very painful process for him but a key moment in his recovery. 'We had to check that there wasn't a build-up of blood, making a barrier that would stop the grafts taking,' explains Dr Al-Najada. He was delighted with what he saw.

As treatment progressed, Ali's condition steadily improved. He was now able to sleep many hours a day on a £70,000 mattress, filled with silicon and sand, that cushioned his back allowing only limited pressure on his burned body. It felt as if he were lying on a bed of air. The air in his room was stirred by a gentle breeze from an air-conditioning unit. The skin on his face now felt cool and fresh, rather than hot and sticky. However, Ali was particularly disturbed by the need to have the dressings changed on a daily basis. 'Every day I was in intensive care I was bored and unhappy,' he recalls. 'I dreaded dressing time.' He also had to endure a lot of injections, some of which enabled the doctors to monitor his blood levels.

Every morning at 8 a.m. he was bathed. 'This was very painful, even with sedatives,' says Mohammed. 'One lady nurse, Stanca, was exceptionally tender with him. She kissed him each time and said, "I promise this won't hurt," and then she kissed him again at the end. He always asked for her.' Ali was beginning to trust the medical team, cooperating more and fighting less when his dressings were changed. One day Ali asked Dr Al-Najada for a spicy shish kebab, his favourite dish. It tasted delicious. 'It's a good sign if he is thinking about food. We want to build him up,' Dr Al-Najada told journalists. Mohammed accompanied the doctor on the kebab-buying expedition, and marvelled at the extent of media interest in Ali. 'The following day, you should have seen the headlines: "Mohammed is seen searching for kebabs for Ali." It was hilarious!' he says, laughing at the memory.

Ali returned to theatre for his second skin-graft operation a week later, on 5 May. Surgery to graft skin from the front of his thighs and right leg on to his lower abdomen lasted two and a half hours. A further five days later he was ready for his fourth and final operation, during which Dr Ghoneim and his assistant surgeon, Dr Raeaf, removed the metal staples holding the skin grafts in place, and grafted a few, small remaining areas.

'All the grafts are healing very nicely indeed,' Dr Al-Najada told journalists a few days later. 'In about a week we will remove all the dressings.' News of Ali's progress was relayed around the world. Under the headline 'Miracle Ali', the *Daily Mirror* said, 'Iraqi missile victim Ali Ismaeel Abbas is making a remarkable recovery after having his final skin graft. Delighted surgeons said he will have hardly any scars despite terrible burns to large areas of his body. The miraculous news comes less than three weeks after doctors in the Iraqi capital Baghdad admitted, "It is probably better if he dies."'

In fact, it is impossible to obtain an entirely seamless join between transplanted skin and the original skin that surrounds it. 'Ali is likely to always have small patches of discoloured skin,' explains Dr Al-Najada. 'It will be possible to see a slight mesh where the skin has been applied. Transplanted skin doesn't grow the way that normal skin grows, so he may have to have surgery to correct that if it becomes uncomfortable.'

Being the centre of so much attention gave Ali strength, but he still suffered bouts of intense depression and despair. 'Everything is finished. No-one will marry me. I can't work. I'm destined to become a beggar,' he told Nafisah Kamal, a gentle physiotherapist wearing a dark grey headscarf who came to introduce herself to him one day.

'Ali had already worked in intensive care with another physiotherapist, Anwar, who had helped him to strengthen his muscles, but I came to tell him that once he left the intensive care unit he would be transferring to me on the ward,' recalls mother of five, Nafisah. 'I found him frustrated and depressed. His spirits were very low.' Ali still felt terribly sad some mornings, but watching cartoons on the DVD player was a distracting way to fill the long hours of seclusion.

As Ali's treatment in the intensive care unit progressed, the doctors began to consider his future. Concentrated physio-therapy as soon as he was well enough to leave intensive care was the obvious short-term goal (Ali would need to learn to walk again having spent so long lying recumbent in bed), but there was also his long-term treatment to consider. Occupational therapy sessions would enable him to retrain his brain to use his nicely shaped feet as substitute hands and his toes as short surrogate fingers. This process would be an important part of his rehabilitation. However, in order to have the best possible chance of gaining full independence it was clear he would benefit from the 'new pair of hands' for which he yearned.

It was also evident to his doctors within the first two weeks of his arrival in Kuwait that the nature of Ali's amputations would require highly specialized prosthetic equipment. The simplest sort of bionic arm is one controlled by the patient's own muscle, and the greater the length of the patient's remaining residual limb, the greater the options for control. Experts in the field of prosthetics prefer to use the term 'residual limb' rather than 'stump'. 'A stump is a useless dead bit of tree,' asserts Diana Morgan. 'But what remains is actually incredibly impor-tant; that's why we call it a residual limb. Without mine I couldn't walk effectively because I wouldn't be able to muscle-power my artificial legs.' Similarly, Ali's residual arms contain the all-important nerve endings that would one day enable him to operate a mechanical arm. Ali's amputations are particularly high – both his arms were burned nearly up to the shoulder – but fortunately a few, precious centimetres of muscle and bone do remain, more so on the right side than the left where his arm was amputated almost to the shoulder. Ali's small residual limbs would prove crucial to his future independence, allowing him to control a custom-built myo-electric limb, an artificial limb controlled by an electric current dictated by impulses from the user. Ali has just enough muscle remaining to allow internal sensors to pick up the slight movements that are the electrical evidence of the user's intention. These muscular twitches communicate a signal to the electronic hand, a state-of-the-art gadget that twists at the wrist and creates a firm grip where thumb and fingers meet. It would take Ali many, many months to learn how to control such a system, but once mastered he would again be independent.

The problem was that myo-electric arms, and the intricate rehabilitative training that goes with them, are not available in Kuwait. Artificial legs can be fitted there, as can cosmetic arms, but to receive the fully functioning bionic upper limbs he craved, it made sense for Ali to be treated in a specialized prosthetic treatment centre. For a boy who had never been out of Iraq, going to Kuwait had been a big adventure: the next stage of his treatment would see him leave the Middle East altogether.

When Ali arrived in Kuwait, the Ministry of Health had begun to receive a number of offers from organizations around the world, keen to be involved in the next stage of Ali's treatment. Some had diplomatic representation. Many came from charities that had collected significant sums of money on Ali's behalf and were understandably keen to spend it on him if they could. E-mails were printed out. Business cards were collected. The details of each offer were carefully collated.

'The trouble we had was how to make up our minds,' recalls Dr Al-Shatti. 'And I wasn't the only one fielding calls: both Dr Ibrahim and Dr Al-Najada were also being approached.'

Therefore, when Zafar Khan, chairman of the UK's Limbless Association, contacted the Kuwaiti Ministry of Health he was just the latest in a long list of interested sponsors. He appreciated that as trustee of the ALI Fund, he would have to do something special to win Ali's trust and keep faith with the thousands of people who had donated money. 'In less than one month we'd raised nearly £270,000,' he recalls. 'At the same time, the Kuwaitis were beginning to think about what to do next for Ali. It seemed the right time to find out how best we could offer our help, and what we should be spending these huge sums on. I felt I could only find out by going there.'

On 4 May 2003 Zafar Khan left London on a Kuwait Airways flight bound for Kuwait City. Surrounded by turbaned Kuwaitis sipping aromatic chai – hot, sweet Arab tea – he was accompanied by a Granada Television crew from ITV's flagship current affairs show, *Tonight With Trevor McDonald*, which had begun making a documentary about Ali.

As Zafar flew towards Kuwait International Airport, he was well prepared. In his briefcase in the overhead locker were materials for his presentation to the doctors on the functional aspects of upper-limb prostheses, and travelling in the darkened belly of the aircraft was a leather holdall, a large bag with a long zip, full of life-enhancing technological magic borrowed from the world's leading rehabilitation centre at Queen Mary's in Roehampton, South London: artificial arms. Nevertheless, he couldn't help feeling slightly apprehensive about the outcome of his pilgrimage. He need not have worried. His visit was destined to be a meeting that Ali Abbas would never forget – not least because the boy would soon discover that he and the intelligent, softly spoken pharmacist shared a profound connection.

In 1966 Zafar Khan was a 21-year-old biochemistry graduate living in his native Pakistan. He had just completed his finals and was about to leave Karachi for the first time to study for a BSc in pharmacy in the UK. On Friday 16 December 1966 he hitched a ride home from Karachi University on the back of a friend's scooter. They were travelling down a narrow road, and had just started over a small, narrow bridge above a dried-up river bed, when they saw a taxi veering towards them from the opposite direction. The car clipped the side of the scooter, fracturing Zafar's right leg and fatally unbalancing the motorcycle. Both men went over the rail. The driver escaped with minor cuts and bruises, but Zafar's compound fracture required urgent medical attention. Unfortunately, the open wound was treated poorly by a trainee doctor at the nearby city centre hospital. Three days after the accident, the wound smelled terrible and his foot had turned black. The plaster was removed and it was evident to the examining doctor that Zafar's leg was decomposing; some of the plaster had seeped into the injury and had caused a serious infection. His terrified parents were gravely told that immediate amputation above the knee was the only option, or gangrene would kill their son.

'I still remember the desperate look in my parents' eyes,' Zafar recalls. 'They wanted to help me but could not do anything to relieve the pain. I had to find the words to ask my mother to allow the surgeons to remove my leg to save my life, but I was lucky to have my parents there: Ali had to cope alone. It is not easy at all to have part of your body removed, especially when it happens to be your hands or your legs. You begin to visualize a life without the part almost immediately, but it is impossible to comprehend the real impact for several years. Trying to adapt to an artificial component in your body, and expecting it to function as normal involves a lifelong process of challenge, disappointment, pain and compromise,' says Zafar who came to the UK eight months after his accident to begin his second degree. After graduating, he registered as a pharmacist in 1971 and worked as a researcher for two large pharmaceutical companies, where he was responsible for a number of patented developments, before setting up the UK's first 24-hour pharmacy in central London to have a rota of private doctors on call. He also found himself increasingly involved in limbless issues, and in March 2002, after three years as vice chairman, had become chairman of the Limbless Association.

Stepping into the international scene after Ali's story became known was a big departure for this tiny charity. 'We felt driven to help Ali, a little boy who has lost not only his arms but his entire family,' Zafar explains. 'We understood well the problems he and the other limbless of Iraq would face. We were the most relevant organization to collect donations, but we had to quickly call an emergency trustees meeting to check whether the constitution of the organization allowed us to work abroad,' he says. Fortunately, it did. The day after Zafar arrived in Kuwait he was joined by Caroline Spelman MP, the then Shadow Secretary of State for International Development, with whom he was also discussing a plan to set up limb-fitting and rehabilitation centres in Iraq. They had first met through their involvement on a project to help landmine victims in Afghanistan. They had hoped to raise money to buy a single ambulance, but their fund-raising efforts were so successful that they were able to buy four.

And so, on 6 May 2003, clutching the precious leather holdall and wearing gown and paper mask, Zafar was among the chattering party of doctors and journalists approaching Ali's private room in the intensive care unit at Ibn Sina Hospital. He was about to offer the boy tangible evidence of his future.

'As I was walking towards his room, I was thinking hard,' recalls Zafar. 'I wasn't sure what I was going to find; and although I knew Ali's face from photographs, I wanted to see how he really looked. When I entered, his head was on the pillow and he turned to look directly at us. I distinctly remember his bright eyes. The other thing that struck me was that he was holding a lovely smile all the time. Then my eyes went to the rest of his body. I could see his remaining very short arm, the right arm, but I couldn't see much of the residual left arm – there wasn't much, I discovered afterwards.'

A translator introduced Ali to Zafar, and explained that he was the chairman of a British charity who had come to visit him to discover how best his organization could provide help for him. The holdall was on the floor. Zafar undid the long zip.

Inside were several artificial arms packed in bubble wrap. He took them out and placed them on the ground, just out of Ali's field of vision. Earlier that morning Ali's doctors and Zafar had had a meeting. 'The doctors weren't sure whether I should show these artificial arms to Ali, what emotional impact they would have on him,' Zafar recalls, explaining that no-one had yet told the boy about the existence of prosthetic arms. 'They were worried about how he would respond, and concerned that they would affect him negatively. As an amputee, I said they could take it from me that losing his arms was the worst shock of his life. Seeing the artificial ones would provide him with hope, not damage him in any way. Also, I wanted him to know what kind of arm he was going to get. I didn't want him to form an impression that artificial arms are like real arms, I wanted him to realize that although they look like flesh and bone there are limitations.'

Once the arms were unwrapped on the floor, Zafar picked the first one up. 'I decided to show him the best looking one, the cosmetic arm, first, to gain his confidence. It looks exactly like your own arm and hand, but it doesn't have any moving parts.'

Ali had never seen a prosthetic limb before. He couldn't believe how realistic it appeared. It even had pores and tiny freckles. The fingernails were particularly amazing, they looked exactly like the genuine article. He now knew for the first time since the accident that he wouldn't have to look different from everyone else. 'It looks just like a real arm,' he told the translator excitedly. 'Will this arm grow?' Zafar explained it would not.

He showed him several other designs before producing his pièce de résistance: the myo-electric arm with its almost bionic function. As Zafar held the forearm, Ali watched in wonder as the fingers and thumb opened and closed, seemingly by themselves. Zafar inserted a pen into the grip, and used the arm to write 'Ali' on the bed sheet.

'He was watching with a lot of interest what this hand could do,' says Zafar. 'Then he asked me, through the translator, a very perceptive question: "OK, it can close, but has it got grip?" He could see that I could hold the pen, but he is very clever and he wanted to know how strong that grip was,' says Zafar. 'So I said, "Well, there is only one way to find out!" and then I grabbed his nose.'

Ali laughed as he felt the sharp pinch of artificial thumb and finger, and sensed the powerful strength of these artificial fingers. He realized this was no toy. 'At that moment I knew that I would be able to eat and drink again,' he says.

The moment was captured on camera by the Granada film crew and photographed by London's *Metro*. Ali's large hazel eyes are brimful of wonder. 'At that moment Ali visibly brightened. It was an amazingly big deal for him. Until that point everyone was still worried about his scars and skin grafts, but this gave him huge confidence. And it needed to come from someone who is in a similar position – only someone like Zafar, who can really understand,' recalls Granada producer Roger Corke.

Uncle Mohammed was also watching Ali's reaction closely. 'I realized just how far Ali had come when he was shown the false arm,' says Mohammed. 'He was grinning from ear to ear.'

It was then that Mr Khan revealed his inspirational trump card. 'Ali had watched as I walked into the room, and of course he wouldn't have realized that I'm an amputee. So I said, "Ali, we have got something in common, you and I. We are both amputees, but we can lead a normal life, I assure you. When I lost my leg, I thought, 'I'm useless. I can't do anything,' but now there is almost nothing I cannot do.'"

Ali couldn't believe this. He'd seen this man walking into the room towards him and he'd never guessed. He seemed completely normal – he didn't even have a stick. 'Can you run?' he asked suddenly. 'Well, that is really the only thing I can't do,' admitted Zafar, who says, 'I explained to him that there are limitations in having an artificial limb, but they do the job. I told him, "I'm alive, I can think – I can do almost everything," and said that being able to perform my daily routine in life makes me very happy.'

Ali had many questions to ask. 'He asked me which leg it was, so I told him the right leg. He then asked if he could see my artificial leg,' recalls Zafar, who says he stood back a little and rolled his trouser up to reveal his flesh-coloured artificial leg. 'I then started to roll it down again, but Ali wasn't ready for that, so I had to roll it back up immediately. He wanted to know how far up the prosthesis went, so I told him above the knee. Then he asked if I could stand on one leg. I said, "Not too long." It is actually very tricky to balance on an artificial leg. Dr Ghoneim realized this, so we cheated a little bit and he stood behind and supported me slightly.'

Throughout the encounter, Ali's eyes shone with concentration. 'He became intensely curious,' recalls Dr Al-Shatti who was also witnessing his delight. 'Ali was asking Zafar, "Can you play? Do you sleep with it on? When do you take it off?" After this, he started to ask questions about what he would himself be able to do. His spirits were very high. He asked if he would be able to write.'

Caroline Spelman was also impressed with Ali's intelligent questions. 'Travelling with Zafar was a very special experience. He was a great inspiration, and we were both immediately struck by Ali. He is a remarkable boy: there is a real sparkle about him. He is highly intelligent and already a consummate politician at the age of 12. He also has a good sense of humour and can be very funny, teasing and joking with the doctors in the hospital. They have all formed a very strong bond with him.'

Unfortunately, the *Metro* photographer's camera flash had been used more or less constantly throughout the encounter. Roger Corke found Ali's reaction to this intrusion quite remarkable. 'He started asking, "What are those pictures going to be used for? Are they going to be used in a good way? Will they help other children?" For a 12-year-old who's lost both his parents and his arms, is burned, traumatized and probably sedated, this struck me as pretty extraordinary. Ali seemed to have an uncanny awareness of the world.'

It was clear to everyone that the meeting with Zafar had profoundly affected Ali. 'It changed him, no doubt about it,' says Dr Al-Najada. 'When he saw the arms with his own eyes, he immediately became much more confident. It was very important to him psychologically and emotionally. Afterwards he kept asking us whether it was really true that he would be able to lead a normal life.'

'When Zafar visited, it changed Ali's life,' agrees Mohammed. 'He became much more optimistic and his appetite improved. As the operations had been carried out, I watched as Ali came back to life. I thought he might die in Kuwait, but he had been reborn. God had taken him from the fire, he had survived the trauma, and now he realized for the first time that he had a future.'

'When I met Zafar, I realized that with the new arms I'd be able to write independently and eat independently again. Seeing him gave me a lot of hope,' says Ali. Soon his excitement had spread all the way to the top. 'A few days after the meeting with Zafar, we interviewed the Kuwaiti Minister of Health, Dr Mohammed Al-Jarralah, for our documentary,' says Roger Corke. 'We were looking for an overview about the situation, but he spent half the time talking about how much hope seeing Zafar's leg and the artificial arms had given Ali.'

Dr Mohammed Al-Jarralah says, 'When Ali saw the artificial limb, the medical team were very impressed with the impact this had on his morale. He kept asking them, "Is it true? That without a limb you can do things, you can survive?"'

Before they left the hospital, the representatives of the Limbless Association met Dr Sabreen Al-Zamil, an assistant reconstructive plastic surgeon. She was determined to tell them about two of her Iraqi child patients who weren't receiving any media attention: a 14-year-old called Ahmed Mohammed Hamza and his six-year-old brother Saad.

Ahmed was born on 31 October 1988, and left school at the age of 12 to work as a shepherd. Iraqi law requires all children to attend school from the age of 6 to 12. Ahmed had been airlifted to Kuwait from a military field hospital near Baghdad after losing his right hand and left leg in a cluster-bomb blast – a ballistic weapon that sprays hundreds of smaller bomblets over a wide area. His sister had been killed, and he had arrived in a critical state before undergoing a series of operations to salvage his remaining right leg, which now has restricted movement. His little brother Saad had lost an eye. The boys didn't know then whether their parents were alive or dead. All they knew was that they had both been injured in the explosion. Dr Sabreen explained that Ahmed was terribly homesick. 'I do not talk about his parents – every time I do, he cries,' she said. 'Ali is probably the most tragic patient we have, but it is very good for people to be aware that he is not the only child that needs help. Many of the other patients would also benefit from artificial limbs.'

'I admired the way Dr Sabreen fought for her patients,' says Caroline Spelman. 'They were both suffering from malnutrition, having lived under sanctions. She was very keen for Ahmed to be brought to London along with Ali, to receive an artificial hand and leg.' Zafar immediately offered to help Ahmed from the fund set up in Ali's name. 'When he walks again, nobody will know he has not got a leg, please tell him' said Zafar, looking at the boy in a wheelchair who looked much younger and smaller than his 14 years.

However, when Zafar Khan and Caroline Spelman left Kuwait, it was clear that neither Ali nor Ahmed would be going anywhere just yet, if at all. Ali was still in intensive care, and the

Kuwaiti Ministry of Health explained that they were unlikely to make a decision about his future care for some weeks. 'It's too early to say where and when Ali will receive new arms,' Dr Al-Najada told journalists. 'But one thing we know is that he will.'

Several other charities had also offered to pay for the next stage of Ali's treatment, offers that also had to be carefully evaluated. And it was still possible that Ali might be treated in Kuwait with imported technology, something that had been raised with Zafar Khan. It was clear that there was not going to be any hasty decision-making.

Nevertheless, as he flew home to London, Zafar felt quite hopeful. He had told the Kuwaiti doctors all about the wonderful facilities at Queen Mary's, Roehampton: the walking school, the prosthetic workshops, and the world-famous rehabilitation centre with its occupational therapy and physiotherapy departments, staffed by dedicated specialists. 'I felt we'd achieved a lot,' he says. 'It was particularly rewarding to see the effect our visit had had on Ali. There are lots of other people I want to help as well – we hope to establish two complete rehabilitation units for the limbless in Iraq, one in Baghdad, the other in Basra – but I felt we had a good chance of being able to help this little boy achieve his potential in life. I really hoped we had done enough.'

Zafar decided to confirm the Limbless Association's offer in writing. In his letter, written on 24 May 2003, he thanked the Kuwaitis for their hospitality and outlined his offer of help, extended initially to both Ali and Ahmed, from the funds raised. 'If you reach a decision that they will stay in Kuwait for further care, then we will be happy to send our prosthetists to Kuwait, to provide training of your prosthetists at Roehampton, and to provide the required artificial limbs and necessary rehabilitation,' he wrote. But because he felt it would be more practical for the boys to come to London for long-term rehabilitation, he focused the remaining three pages of his letter on the intricate details of the care they would receive in the UK. 'The prosthetists at Roehampton have years of experience of providing services to children similar to Ali and Ahmed. All members of our multi-disciplinary team have been following Ali's progress, and they know that they would be able to help. One of the prosthetists speaks fluent Arabic. We will also try very hard to match the love and affection that you have provided to them in Kuwait.' He addressed practical issues such as living arrangements, schooling and support within a Muslim framework. He also emphasized that amputees need lifelong care and attention, and that the commitment from the Limbless Association would be for life. 'We would be happy to support their stay in the UK if they decide to remain here throughout.' He also pointed out that the proposed rehabilitation centres in Iraq would be expected to be up and running within one to two years, and that the Kuwaitis would be welcome to send staff for training in the UK, giving Ali and Ahmed a range of choices for their future. 'I very much hope that the contents of this letter will be of use to you. Yours sincerely, Zafar Khan.'

It was to be three long months before he would receive an official reply.

CHAPTER THIRTEEN

Ali's First Painting

'When I was out of intensive care I got more of a chance to see other people. I spoke to families from Kuwait and that really lifted my morale. Nafisah – my physiotherapist – took me on several outings in her Porsche. We went to the zoo, to an adventure playground, and to an aquarium where I saw sharks. I was very excited about the fact that I had a ride with my physiotherapist in the most expensive car in Kuwait. I felt so proud of myself I found I couldn't stop talking about it.

'Nafisah helped me a lot and made me do things that at the time I found difficult and didn't want to do very much, but she insisted that it was for the best. Learning to use my feet was difficult at first. I was still hoping to one day have limbs, but first she taught me so many things: how to take off my T-shirt, how to write, how to play Play Station. She even tried to teach me how to thread a needle, but I said, "No, I won't be able to do that – I don't like sewing!"'

Ali Ismaeel Abbas

On 13 May 2003 Ali Abbas was finally released from imprisonment. His skin grafts were healing beautifully and he was allowed to leave intensive care. Ali was happy to be leaving his sterile room after nearly a month and moving into a private room in the male burns unit. Being in isolation wasn't much fun, and talking to people through a glass screen by telephone was a novelty that had worn off. He enjoyed talking Arabic with the nurses as they washed him; now he hoped for a bit more variety.

'I was so happy for Ali when he left intensive care,' says his uncle Mohammed, who had been offered the next-door room to Ali, even though he wasn't a patient. 'He looked and felt so much better, and as well as more freedom it meant that he would need to have fewer invasive procedures.' The move also represented greater freedom for Mohammed, who had dutifully stayed by Ali's side for up to 18 hours a day for the past four weeks.

Ali was now able to meet some of the other Iraqi children who had also been brought to Kuwait. They were receiving the same treatment, but not the same publicity. They included Ali Hussein, an articulate, angry and highly intelligent six-year-old whose face had been destroyed by a bomb attack, leaving him blind in one eye. He was undergoing extensive plastic surgery to rebuild his face, with part of his forehead being used to build a new nose. Four-year-old Farah Arkan had suffered burns to both arms and both her parents had been killed. He also met six-year-old Saad and his brother Ahmed, who was destined to become Ali's great friend and ally. There was a two-year age difference between the boys, but shepherd and school-boy were soon to discover that they shared an impish sense of humour, and a future.

Ali had been lying on his back constantly for nearly seven weeks. The muscles in his legs and abdomen were now very weak. He was bedridden: he could neither walk nor sit. He felt there was very little he could do. Even his excitement about the prospect of artificial arms had faded a little.

'Hello Ali, how are you? I think we already met in intensive care. I'm here to work with you.' The sing-song voice belonged to Nafisah, the physiotherapist with the dark grey headscarf whom he had met a few weeks earlier. Ali grunted an uninvolved hello, and continued to stare at the ceiling. He really couldn't be bothered. 'What do you want me to do? My life is finished,' he said.

'Well, Ali, what do you want to do?'

This seemed like a different sort of question. He brightened for the first time that morning. 'I want to run.'

'That would certainly be possible, Ali.'

'Really?'

'I promise.'

'Well, if you promise that I can run, then I want to stand up today,' he said, looking at Nafisah directly for the first time. 'OK, but first we are going to work together for a little while,' she said levelly. With 11 years' experience in her field, nine of them in the burns and plastic surgery unit at Ibn Sina, the 37-year-old physiotherapist wasn't about to be fazed by a 12-year-old boy. She was used to the depression, anger, despair and bitterness of burns patients: she had also watched the majority of them rediscover their passion and enthusiasm for life once they embarked on a course of rehabilitation and began to feel truly supported. It was just a question of finding a way to latch on.

'The first time I worked with Ali he wouldn't obey anything: he was trouble,' recalls Nafisah. 'We worked together for three hours and it was hard going. I knew that he had to learn to trust me, and the best way to do that was for us to achieve everything I promised. It was actually a little bit too early for Ali to stand – I normally wait longer: perhaps three or four days – but Ali in particular needed some instant results to increase his confidence.'

At the end of the day, Mohammed and Nafisah helped him into a bright red wheelchair and, as he gritted his teeth, they put their arms around him and raised him slowly to a standing position. Ali then asked to try again, by himself. He found it almost impossible to raise himself to standing, and could feel the scar tissue pulling all over his body. He forced himself to keep going. 'I feel really dizzy,' he whispered. 'I'm going to fall down.'

'Don't worry: just shout out if you need to and I will put you down safely,' said Nafisah. A few moments later Ali was standing alone, wobbling slightly, but smiling broadly for the first time in weeks. He looked triumphant. 'Ali, you did it! Well done!' cried Nafisah. She could also see that he was an extremely determined young man. 'He is very intelligent. I knew then that I could capture him.'

Nafisah continued to involve Ali fully in his rehabilitation from those first important moments. 'It was important that if I said he could do something, that he managed to achieve it; so I made him take an equal part in his treatment,' she says. 'But when I asked him what would he like to do in the future, he put his head down. I said, "Don't do that: I want you to be proud of yourself. Put your head up and talk to me." Then he told me sadly, "Before, I was thinking of being a soldier, but now, without hands, I can't do anything." I said this was nonsense and started to tell him lots of stories about people who have lost their hands and feet and gone on to achieve all sorts of things. I said, "Ali, you still have your brain; you only lost your hands," and he replied, "Well, I could be a translator: I can learn English: I can learn anything. But I don't want to be a doctor – I've seen how much pain they have to make."'

The next day Nafisah and Ali drew up a chart of goals and plans. 'He said "We'll really do all this?" and I reassured him that together we certainly would.' Ali told Nafisah that he really wanted to be able to pray, but that he couldn't because he couldn't sit down by himself. 'I said, "Don't worry: I will help you."' All day long Ali practised lowering himself into different-sized chairs, some low, some high. Without arms, his centre of gravity had risen, and he needed to learn to balance all over again. It took a lot of concentration, particularly as his abdominal muscles were still extremely weak. To Nafisah's amazement, at the end of the day Ali was able to lower himself all the way to the floor with her support. It was difficult because he had to fold his legs up at just the right moment in order to maintain his balance.

'The next day he came to me in the morning and told me he'd just sat down by himself. I couldn't believe it,' she says. Perhaps Ali was inspired to push himself that particular morning, having talked to one of his sisters and an aunt for the first time since leaving Baghdad. Uncle Mohammed held the phone to Ali's ear during the 30-minute chat. Soon Ali was sobbing with emotion as they told him all the news from home, and he told them about the hospital and all the gifts he had received. 'Somebody from the US sent me a nice football,' Ali recalls. 'I really enjoyed playing with it. I used to ask the nurse to bring it to my legs so I could kick it, or sometimes I'd head-kick it. It was amazing to talk to my family. I missed them a lot.'

One week after he left intensive care, Ali's dressings were removed. 'I was very, very, very happy and relieved when they took the dressing off for the final time,' remembers Ali. 'The skin looked much better than I thought it would.' The new skin was very itchy, however; so each day he was treated with soothing cream, and he also underwent a programme of gentle stretching exercises to help the scar tissue become more flexible. Measurements were taken for the pressure garment Ali would have to wear constantly over his trunk and legs for the next two years. Made from an elastic, skin-coloured fabric, this tight, zipped garment applies continuous pressure to scar tissue and stops it from developing into lumpy patches of raised skin. The downside is that it can take some getting used to. 'I hated it when I first got it,' Ali remembers with a shudder. 'I used to cry each time they put it on. But after a few weeks I could already see what good it had done my body. The skin looks much smoother and nicer. Now I ask for it to be put on. I have to wear it all the time, but it's taken off when I bathe.'

Mohammed and Ali had also been befriended by Mohammed Al-Bader, a cheerful, 39-year-old, Kuwaiti air traffic controller who had started to visit every day. 'I am just one of thousands of people who were touched by Ali's story, but I was lucky because he was in my country,' explains this father of four. 'Ali always smiled and was nice to visitors even though he was still in discomfort. Ali's uncle told me that Ali cries every night, sad memories would attack him without mercy while he slept, so during my visits I tried to concentrate on supporting him psychologically. His uncle was worried that he still wasn't eating enough. We all know children like fast food. We know it's not healthy, but I decided to bring him a burger like the ones my own children like. I was delighted to see him eat it, so from that day on we started ordering restaurant food. I also found him a can of Iraqi pickles that he likes.'

Feeding Ali had become a symbolic way of showing him love. 'One day two nice Syrian ladies came to visit him,' says Mohammed Al-Bader. 'They brought him a lot of food and sweets, and started to feed him. But Ali had just eaten his lunch. Ali did not tell them he was full up, because he is a polite and shy boy, so I told them. On the way to the lift I saw one of the Syrian ladies crying at Ali's pain. Ali makes the whole world cry.'

His days on the burns ward took on a predictable shape: two sessions of physio – one in the morning; one at the end of the day – and a daily visit from one of the plastic surgeons. 'I always gave Ali some control over our sessions,' explains Nafisah. 'I tried to be sensitive to his mood. I didn't push him because I didn't want him to hate the treatment. We needed to work together, not against each other.' Unfortunately, he still had to wash every day, but later on he was allowed in a bubbling hydrotherapy bath to help soften his scars.

As Ali's scars began to heal, Nafisah concentrated on building up the muscles in his weakened and damaged torso. 'Every time we started a new thing he didn't want to learn – he didn't trust himself,' she recalls. 'I would always tell him, "It will be difficult, but you have to try, or you won't be able to do anything." Each day we did simple things that would give him a sense of achievement. We always finished the day trying something harder.' Sometimes, overnight, Ali's brain would subconsciously assimilate the harder task, and in the morning he amazed even himself by being able to do it effortlessly.

One morning Nafisah showed him a small device she'd made. It was a Velcro loop that could be fastened to his residual right arm. A soft plastic tube was attached to the loop, into which a piece of cutlery could be pushed, enabling Ali to feed himself. 'I strapped it on and showed him how it worked and immediately he started bashing his head on the fork.' For the first time since the accident he was able to scratch himself. 'Everybody else does this for me,' he said cheerfully.

At the end of May he was ready to take his first tentative steps. Uncle Mohammed helped him to his feet. Ali grimaced in pain; then gingerly tested out his frail legs. As he took a few slow steps, he gave a gentle smile of victory: another milestone, another flurry of excited headlines. But as he walked up a short flight of steps to a downward ramp he felt himself swaying disconcertingly: he felt terribly wobbly. 'It was difficult learning to walk again because I'd spent a long time in bed,' he recalls. 'I wanted to walk, but I felt very tired. When I put my feet on the floor they had pins and needles, and it was like they were about to slip, and they were cold. I was feeling dizzy. Without the arms I felt like jelly.'

It wasn't surprising that walking felt so peculiar to Ali, and not just because the muscles in his legs had wasted during eight weeks of inactivity. Our arms normally provide us with two opposing weights that we use to regain our balance if we start to topple over. A tightrope walker's pole follows the same principle: if he starts to fall to the right, dipping the pole to the left helps him to regain his balance. But Ali now had to learn to compensate for his missing arms by devising new strategies with Nafisah's encouragement that would allow him to feel safely balanced during daily life. For this reason he soon developed a tendency to stoop when he walked, but Nafisah continually corrected him. Bad posture wasn't the solution.

'In a few days you'll be able to walk much better,' Dr Al-Najada told him. 'In a couple of weeks you'll be running in the corridors.' Ali says his prophecy was correct. 'It took me 10–15 days before I could walk normally again,' he says. 'I practised every day.' To build up his strength he also began using an exercise bike.

When it came to picking things up, Ali instinctively compensated for his lack of arms by using his teeth and lips as substitute thumb and forefinger, but Nafisah soon started encouraging him to try something different. 'You can't use your mouth for everything: some things are too dirty,' she said. 'I can teach you to write, Ali,' she said.

'How come?'

'You have to learn to compensate. I will teach you to use your feet.'

Ali shook his head. It hardly seemed necessary. He would have new arms before too long, after all.

'Listen, you don't know what will happen in the future, so don't only depend on the arms. You have to be independent,' Nafisah urged him. Soon Ali was bravely attempting to angle a pen between his toes. After a few hours, he was able to write his name.

Ali soon discovered he had a natural facility for using his feet. He started by trying to pick up wooden blocks, and then dropping them into a box. He and Nafisah made a game of this every morning for a week. He then practised threading nuts on to bolts driven through a piece of wood, rotating his ankles to help his toes get a better purchase on the shiny metal. Soon he had mastered the art of stacking plastic cups inside one another.

As the weeks went by, Ali's fine control over his toes quickly improved. Soon he was mastering quite complex operations and using his toes like true surrogate fingers. He was able to pick up clothes pegs and to press the mechanism open by forcing his big toe against its neighbour, before attaching the pegs, one after another, to a vertical stick. Intensive physiotherapy coupled with a child's natural flexibility meant he was soon so adept that he could hold cutlery in his toes and feed himself. He was even learning to play computer games with his feet – competing, inevitably, against Ahmed, with whom he was forming a close alliance and who was also learning to adapt to his missing hand and foot.

The brain of a child is particularly adaptable to changes in the body's physical circumstances. As Ali's brain receives increased sensory input from his toes, its neural networks begin slowly to adjust. This 'plasticity' in the brain means that Ali's toes will one day provide the sort of detailed, three-dimensional feedback that most of us take for granted from our fingers.

The tasks helped Ali towards independence, but they had a secondary purpose. 'My main goal was to help him become independent, with or without artificial limbs. That's why I taught him to use his feet and toes,' explains Nafisah. They were also mini workouts that helped to restore the normal range of motion in his joints, built up his wasted muscle and prevented a build-up of scar tissue from impeding his movement.

By early June Ali was feeling much more positive. 'I'm OK now: the burns healed and I'm just waiting for my new arms,' he told journalists brightly. Mohammed felt that his progress was just like the miracle Dr Al-Najada had anticipated. 'Ali is in high spirits. He's no longer in pain,' Mohammed told reporters.

'He moves around, he sees his friends, he watches television – he's just like any other kid.'

Ali felt equally positive about his progress towards independence. After hours of practice, he was now able to control a pen deftly between his toes. Each letter was still a great exercise in concentration, but they were gradually getting smaller and neater. On 8 June, while he was writing his name, he was visited by some Kuwaiti schoolchildren and their English teacher who was particularly fascinated as she watched Ali controlling a pen so artfully. 'Why doesn't he paint some pictures? We'll make it into a card and we'll give Ali the profits,' she said. Nafisah put the suggestion to Ali. 'He was very excited at the thought of making money from paintings,' Nafisah recalls. 'He immediately went to his room to get his own supplies, the art materials that people had sent him and that so far he hadn't wanted to use.'

Nafisah filled a jar with water as Ali sat down on his soft mat. First he dipped his paintbrush into the water, then he chose a rich brown from the watercolour palette. Shifting his position slightly, he pulled his foot over the paper and made two confident vertical lines down the centre. He then rinsed the paintbrush in the water by carefully jiggling his foot about, before picking a vibrant green and making zigzag palm leaves. He completed his painting with a few coconuts, some birds and a couple of bright blue clouds. Everyone agreed that this was a significant – and rather masterful – piece of work.

From then on Ali started painting regularly, always choosing vibrant colours and, curiously, often painting palm trees. Nafisah took him to task over this. 'It's all I've ever seen. It's all I know!' he explained. The cards were duly printed by the British Ladies Society of Kuwait. A selection of Ali's paintings appear on the front of the small, professionally printed cards. On the backs is a colour photo of Ali painting, and a short summary of his story, together with a note about donations: 'Ali learned to paint with his feet only 16 weeks following the tragedy,' the text states proudly.

Mohammed Al-Bader, the air traffic controller, brought in his laptop and showed Ali, who had never seen a computer before, how to use it. 'I showed him the digital photographs I'd taken of him, and then I let him try using the mouse with his foot. He wasn't bad for a beginner. I believe that working in computers is one option for Ali's future.'

Throughout his physiotherapy Ali was still visited every day by Dr Al-Najada and Dr Ghoneim, who carefully monitored his healing skin grafts. By early June Dr Al-Najada was able to report, 'All the grafts were excellent: the grafts healed; the donor area healed.' He was also advising Mohammed on a daily basis. An odd assortment of foreigners were vying to be part of the boy's future, and some journalists had started offering money for interviews. Mohammed found the politics of the situation perplexing. He definitely wanted Ali to benefit from the attention, as any loving relative would, but he certainly wasn't 'demanding payment' as several media reports have erroneously claimed. 'It is untrue that Mohammed was only giving interviews for money. I know, because he gave me one,' says the documentary film-maker, Roger Corke, who had been following Ali's story closely since Zafar Khan's visit.

Meanwhile, Mohammed asked Ahmed about his parents and where he was from, but the boy seemed confused and any mention of his life in Iraq upset him terribly. After a few days, Mohammed decided to write a letter to Ahmed's missing father. 'Your sons are in Kuwait, they are doing well – perhaps you will be able to join them here soon,' he wrote. The letter was passed on to the Red Cross who had been trying to locate Ahmed's and Saad's parents for the past six weeks. Finally, in May, the boy's father received wonderful news – a letter from Mohammed that told him that his sons, Ahmed and Saad, were alive and well.

CHAPTER FOURTEEN

'They Start to Love me'

'Why do they want to make TV and write about me and
send me presents? It's because of what happened to me
during the war, the injuries and all that. People feel sorry
for me for what I lost, for my family and my arms. They
start to love me because of what happened to me. Without
them I wouldn't have got as far as I have now. But I would
rather not have fame. I would rather be normal and
nobody.'

Ali Ismaeel Abbas

While Ali was concentrating on learning to walk again, building
up his muscles with short walks around his hospital room, the
public appetite for information about him continued unabated.
Soon he had received a blizzard of promises from foreign
celebrities, charities and the media.

Ali and Mohammed listened quietly as Dr Al-Najada tried to
explain media reports that there would be a huge benefit concert
for him in the US, a Hollywood film of his life, Canadian
passports for his family and stories that he was about to fly to
Europe or America for treatment. 'Almost all those reports were
wrong – the Kuwaiti doctors and government officials caring for
him were still weeks away from any decision on his future,' says

Peter Wilson, the Australian journalist who had helped arrange Ali's evacuation to Kuwait.

As well as Zafar Khan's British offer, Ali now had open invitations for the next stage of treatment from countries including Italy, Spain, Greece, Australia, the US and Canada. A few days after Zafar's visit, Elissa Montanti, the head of a small American charity called the Global Medical Relief Fund, had arrived in Kuwait hoping to take Ali to the US. She came bearing return air tickets, a Nintendo Game Boy computer, and a signed photo and a letter from Arnold Schwarzenegger, just weeks before he announced his political ambitions: 'You are an extremely brave and special young man. My thoughts and prayers are with you. Stay strong. Your friend, Arnold.' Ali struggled to place the Hollywood star, but the *Terminator* poster looked familiar. The doctors explained he wasn't ready to go anywhere.

He was also visited in June by Dr Faleh Hafuth, an Iraqi surgeon living in Ontario, Canada, who had fled Saddam Hussein's regime in 1988 after being arrested and imprisoned as a political prisoner. Dr Hafuth, the vice-president of the Canadian Iraqi Society, made an offer for Ali to come to Canada to live with him, his wife Bothaya and their three young children. He said he was even willing to adopt Ali legally into his family. But Dr Hafuth quickly discovered that his well-intentioned invitation, made initially by phone to Ali's uncle Mohammed and with a promise to support visa applications for his remaining family, was much more difficult to realize than he had envisaged. 'The problem with Dr Hafuth's offer from our point of view', says Dr Al-Shatti at the Kuwaiti Ministry of Health, 'was that we never received anything in writing.' Nevertheless, for many weeks Ali and Mohammed continued to discuss the possibility of making a new life in Canada with the good doctor.

In the UK, money was still being collected in Ali's name.

London's *Evening Standard* raised more than £300,000 for the Red Cross, which spent the money on providing clean water and generators for hospitals; the *Daily Mirror*'s Ali Appeal had also reached six figures; the Limbless Association's ALI Fund was still growing by the day: Steven Dickson of Dickson's Newsagents in Wincanton plastered a board in his shop window with newspaper cuttings about Ali and put a tin on his counter; a group of American schoolchildren, whose teacher wears a prosthetic leg, collected one-cent pieces in large water jugs, raising over £300, and sent their teacher to the charity's office in Roehampton, to deliver it personally; and in Worcester, Cornel Hrisca-Munn, an 11-year-old Romanian boy adopted by a British couple as a baby, raised more than £4000 for Ali and the other children injured in the war by swimming 50 lengths in his local pool. This was a particularly generous act: Cornel was born with severely shortened arms and had to have his right leg amputated at birth.

By now Thomas Edwards, the charismatic Mancunian burger van man, had the direct number to Ali's room and was communicating regularly with Ali, who had started calling him 'my English uncle'. The conversations were translated by one of Ali's favourite nurses, Abner Mayol, with whom Thomas had soon struck up a bond. Thomas relayed every detail of Ali's progress to Diana Morgan, chief executive of the Limbless Association. And when Abner and Mohammed sent Thomas some photographs of Ali he sent her those as well. Diana and Zafar were working hard in the background on Ali's case, as well as attending to the needs of Britain's 62,000 amputees, so his day-to-day help was appreciated. The photographs were passed on to the prosthetic engineers at Queen Mary's, who studied them for additional insights into his physical condition. Thomas also recorded a video about his life in Manchester and posted it to the Gulf state. 'I wanted him to see what England was like,' he says of the video that also included footage of his glass display cabinet where two photos of Ali were proudly on display. 'Abner told me that when Mohammed saw that video the look in his eyes changed. It made a big impression on him. And after they'd finished watching it, Abner phoned and said, "Mohammed now says he wants to go to the UK. Do you know if the offer from the Limbless Association is still on?" I told him that I thought it definitely was.'

One afternoon in the middle of June, when Ali was being put through his paces by Nafisah, an elegant journalist with a husky Irish accent stepped quietly into the treatment room. Andrea Catherwood, ITN's international correspondent, had last seen the little boy two months earlier as she held him down as he was washed in the squalor of a Baghdad hospital. 'It was two months since I'd last seen him on that chaotic night. I remembered well how tiny and vulnerable he seemed; but as I walked into the room and saw him sitting and playing, well, he just looked like a completely different child. The contrast was amazing. He was so big and active and he no longer had these massive eyes. He looked like a 12-year-old without arms, rather than like a terribly ill, mutilated body.'

Ali was eager to demonstrate his new skills to Andrea and the producer of the Granada documentary, Roger Corke. He had rediscovered his old mischievousness. 'Over the next couple of days Ali was into everything,' Andrea recalls. 'He would play until he was exhausted.' He ran confidently up and down the corridors of the hospital, opening doors with his teeth and feet. He encouraged Andrea's crew to teach him how to operate a video camera with his toes, albeit with rather shaky results, and he peered deep into the lens, watching his reflection thoughtfully. His football was constantly being kicked up and down the ward. 'I think I could become a footballer because they mainly use their feet,' Ali said as he booted the ball through the door frame into the ward. 'David Beckham sent me a T-shirt, you know; I would love to meet him and I would love to play for Manchester United,' he shouted.

His physiotherapist delighted in his exuberance. To Nafisah it was the best possible result from the hours of work she had put into increasing his confidence. 'I always knew I could capture him because he is very intelligent and so determined. Once he was out of danger and started rehab, his own spirit had begun to take over and he and Ahmed were becoming increasingly lively,' recalls Nafisah fondly. 'They were always playing: Ali would push Ahmed's wheelchair around the place. Ali was always coming to tell me about all the bad things they had done. Ali would ambush the nurses; the other boys would chase them.' They managed to break a lift by pressing too many buttons, and soon Ali was building up his strength by tripping up the nurses.

'Oh yes,' says Ali, laughing when taken to task about this. 'In the hospital we used to do a lot of practical jokes on the nurses because we love them. It's like a joke – we only do it because we like them so much,' he says with a sweet smile.

Even Mohammed wasn't immune to the pranks of Ali and Ahmed. One day he awoke to find his bed in an unfamiliar corridor – while he was asleep the boys had released the brake on his bed and rolled him out of his room. And they were forever calling him on his mobile phone when he was in the bathroom. Ali had also become very attached to a small teddy bear called Nourson that belonged to Catherine Ecolivet, the French missionary. One of his favourite games was to pick up Nourson, or 'baby' as he renamed him, with his toes and hide him in the burns unit, his hiding places becoming increasingly obscure. 'I soon learned that when Ali or Ahmed said with a large smile "Where is the baby?" that Nourson was in trouble somewhere,' laughs Catherine. 'Ali and Ahmed are very creative!'

Producer Roger Corke was also struck by the difference in Ali since he had last seen him in intensive care. 'The first few times you see a TV camera crew it's exciting, but he'd realized that it could actually be rather tedious – particularly if you'd rather be playing. He had a lot of fight and gumption, and made it quite clear when he'd had enough of us!' Roger, governor of a primary school in Oxfordshire, also took a role in the ongoing negotiations over Ali's future. 'The choice at this point appeared to be between Canada and the UK,' he says. 'In Canada the offer had come from an individual: there was no back-up from a charity. I wanted Mohammed and Ali to know what the UK had to offer, but it wasn't my job to put the case.' So, when he overheard one of the medical staff, Nabil, discussing the Canadian offer with Mohammed, Roger immediately telephoned Zafar Khan, who was working day and night behind the scenes, and suggested he talk to Mohammed, using Nabil as an interpreter. For the next 45 minutes Zafar was able to discuss details of the British offer directly with Mohammed.

A few days after Roger Corke and Andrea left Kuwait, Mohammed received some exciting news. 'I spoke to my wife and she told me that she was several months pregnant,' he says. 'I was overjoyed. We hadn't had a child for 12 years and I really wanted another baby, so this was a happy accident.' The news also caused him to reflect on the long separation his care for Ali had created. 'Although I have been away before, on national service, it was usually only for about three weeks at most. I miss my wife and family, and find our separation very difficult, but I have patience to look after Ali because of what he's been through. He feels as much like my child as my own son.'

Nafisah had also become very attached to Ali, and they had developed a tactile and loving relationship. 'He really has something. You can't help but be drawn to him,' she says. Yet this was the physiotherapist who told Dr Al-Shatti that before the war she would never have dreamed of talking to an Iraqi citizen, let alone treating or helping one. 'Before meeting Ali, I never imagined that I would be able to help an Iraqi,' she says. 'I obviously have a duty to treat all patients, whatever their nationality, so you have to set that aside – but I had soon become closer to Ali than to any other patient, Iraqi or Kuwaiti, in my entire career. I gave him my whole energy and treated him like another son. We had two sessions a day, but I wanted to work longer with him. After work, I invited him to sit in our staff room, where he would draw or tell jokes. We would sit together and talk about all sorts of things. He showed me the photographs of his parents and I could see how poor they were, how they had absolutely nothing. One day he told me, "Dr Nafisah, you gave me hope." Ali is the sort of patient you can never forget.'

In July Dr Al-Najada told Ali that he had a gift to give him: Ali was now well enough to leave the hospital for the first time. 'I'm an Iraqi. I've always dreamed of seeing Kuwait,' said Ali excitedly. When he was asked who he would like to accompany him he immediately asked for Nafisah. 'She taught me everything,' the boy explained. Now he wanted her to show him her city.

Nafisah had already introduced him to her youngest children and her husband. Now she took him to her home – something she had never done with a patient before. 'In the hospital Ali had met my two youngest children: my daughter Shaayma, who is 9, and my 11-year-old son, Talib. But when Ali came to my house he met my 17-year-old twin daughters and my 16-year-old son. He joked with me then, "Doctor, you've cheated me: I thought all the time you are young, but you are not."' As she cooked lunch, she heard peals of laughter as Ali and her son Talib played computer games. 'Ali was winning all the time,' she says.

Soon Ali had been to an aquarium and had visited shops and restaurants. He had also seen the sea for the first time, and eaten ice cream. He had made telephone calls on Nafisah's mobile and had had his curly hair cut short at a proper barber's shop. One

149

day Nafisah's family took him to Entertainment City, a vast theme park of dodgems and roller-coaster rides where it was possible to take pot shots at cartoons of Saddam Hussein on the Wild West shooting gallery. The theme park is just a few hundred yards from Camp Doha, the American military base where 10,000 troops had prepared for war.

Ali relished his new-found freedom and the chance to play outside again, away from the restrictive hospital environment. 'I took him out on three trips with my family and some of the other staff,' says Nafisah. 'I wanted him to see as much as possible of Kuwait City because I thought he would probably be leaving us soon.'

CHAPTER FIFTEEN

Two Boys Together

'Ahmed and I are very good friends, first of all because he's Iraqi, and second of all because he used to come to my room when I was out of intensive care. He came to visit me with a can of Pepsi and some sweets and seeds, and I thought it was a party.

'Then one day Ahmed suggested this idea: "Ali, why don't you and I go to Canada and get treated together?" So I said, "Yeah, that's a good idea. I'll ask my uncle." Canada was on offer and my uncle said, "Well, that's a good idea actually; I'll ask the doctor who's offering the thing in Canada." So he went and asked him and the doctor said, "Well, I can't help Ahmed. I can only help Ali. I've already started the paperwork for Ali, so I can't really do anything for Ahmed." My uncle came back and told us the news, so Ahmed said, "OK, why don't we go to the UK so we can be together?" I said, "Well, if he [the doctor in Canada] isn't helping you, then we'll go to Britain instead."

'We keep asking ourselves, "What if we hadn't been together? What if we were in different countries? What would we have done? Thank God we're together, but what if we weren't? What would we have done by ourselves in a country that's totally different to ours?"'

Ali Ismaeel Abbas

On 1 July 2003, the same day David Beckham arrived in Spain to scenes of wild hysteria, following his £25 million transfer to Real Madrid, a small charity in south-west London discovered that they were also going to receive two very special guests. For the past three months the Kuwaiti government had carefully considered all the offers received for the next stage of Ali's treatment. On 26 July the Kuwaiti prime minister officially announced that Ali Ismaeel Abbas and Ahmed Mohammed Hamza were to be treated in the UK at Queen Mary's Hospital, Roehampton – one of the world's leading centres for prosthetics and rehabilitation.

'I was particularly struck by Zafar Khan when we met,' explains Dr Al-Shatti. 'As a disabled man he understands the issues Ali will face and he was very sincere. He was prepared to make the entire fund raised available for Ali's future, and he was committed to taking Ahmed as well, which we felt would be important for both boys. They are very cheerful together, and from the early days they were always laughing and teasing one another. Together they make a joyful friendship and have a lot of fun, tricks and jokes. The company and support they offer each other is a very effective form of psychotherapy. They have both suffered a double tragedy: their physical injuries and the loss of family members.'

Another thing the British offer had going for it was location. 'London is much closer to Baghdad than America or Canada, so it would be easier for Ali to visit his family,' says Dr Al-Shatti. 'Furthermore, when I did some homework at our artificial limb centre in Kuwait there was a consensus that Ali would be served best by this choice.'

Some people believe it is only right that Ali should receive treatment in one of the countries responsible for the missile attack that injured him and killed his family, but quite apart from the British public's generosity in raising such huge sums for Ali, there are also medical reasons underpinning the decision –

as well as something of a historical tradition. The close ties between Britain and Kuwait – where English is widely spoken – go back more than 200 years, and for many years the Kuwaitis have relied upon UK expertise for advanced prosthetic treatment. Several of their prosthetists had also trained at Queen Mary's.

The hospital has an international reputation as a centre of excellence, having worked with amputees since the First World War. 'War accelerates technology,' explains Diana Morgan. 'Roehampton has seen amputees through two world wars and numerous other conflicts, and therefore the level of knowledge here is amongst the best in the world. Provision of artificial limbs restores independence and dignity.'

The words of Private F. W. Chapman of the 23rd Royal Welch Fusiliers, a serviceman who had lost both arms in combat, provided the inspiration that gave birth to Queen Mary's Hospital in 1915. The founder, Mary Eleanor Gwynne Holford, was walking through the wards at Millbank Military Hospital just after Britain's first exchange of prisoners of war with Germany, when she saw the armless man sitting at a table with 'a look of utter sadness and hopelessness' on his face.

'In front of him lay what the Government had given him as a substitute for these arms: two leather sockets with hooks attached. I bent down and asked him to tell me his story. He looked up at me and said, "Is this all my country can do for me?" I then and there made a vow that I would work for one object and that was to start a hospital whereby all those who had the misfortune to lose a limb in this terrible war could be fitted with those most perfect artificial limbs human science could devise,' Mrs Gwynne Holford said later.

In all, over 41,000 officers and men lost limbs in the First World War, of whom two-thirds were supplied with artificial limbs at Roehampton. There were approximately half the number of amputation cases in the Second World War, due to advances in surgical technique, better treatment of infection and the wider existence of blood transfusions.

Before the First World War, amputation and limb-fitting were totally separate processes. When an amputee, following amputation, had been discharged by his surgeon he had to purchase an artificial limb, often from an American catalogue. Roehampton pioneered the idea that the surgeon should recommend whatever limb was most suited to a particular patient, and that it should be fitted under the surgeon's supervision – also that the patient should be trained in its use before leaving the hospital. This rehabilitative approach remains central to the work of the hospital today.

Over the next few years workshops were built at Queen Mary's so that the limb-makers could be based on site. And although the raw materials – usually wood and acetone – were still fairly basic, at last the patients were close enough to the technicians to enable a degree of customization to enter the technology.

Queen Mary's has been at the forefront of artificial arm technology since its inception. Writing in the June 1921 edition of *Modern Artificial Limbs*, C. Jennings Marshall, the assistant surgeon to King's College Hospital, explained:

> While the function of a lost lower limb has for centuries been capable of replacement with a fair degree of success, the achievements with the arm have remained on a very much less satisfactory basis. The work of the arm-training centre at Roehampton is an object-lesson in successful methods of overcoming such problems. The patient begins to understand that restoration of function is taken for granted as a thing beyond doubt. He is able to go freely anywhere, seeing armless men at work – digging, hoeing, using a pitchfork, wheeling a barrow even up an acute slope – and doing all these things without effort or

discomfort. He can see men hold a cricket bat, drive a golf ball, play billiards. It will not be long before the athlete will find that there is no need for armless men to forego the pleasures he derived from sport.

In 1942 children were treated at Queen Mary's for the first time, and, 17 years later, the hospital treated over 80 per cent of all UK babies affected by thalidomide, victims of the drug given to their mothers during pregnancy that created a generation of babies born without arms.

It was clear that Ali was going to the best possible destination, a hospital where injuries of his type are dealt with on a regular basis and where the technology he required had been born. He and Ahmed were overjoyed that they would be able to stay together. Ali's uncle Mohammed was also happy with the outcome: 'I originally had Canada in mind, but the doctors advised me we'd be better off in England. The offer from the Limbless Association was much more tangible and organized,' he says. And it now seemed likely that Ahmed's father, Mohammed Hamza, was coming to join them. Saad, his six-year-old, had already returned home to Iraq; now, with the help of the Red Cross, Mr Hamza began to make plans to join his eldest son in Kuwait.

The State of Kuwait had paid the full cost of Ali's treatment so far, as well as that of the other Iraqi children injured in the war. Now the government announced that they would continue to fund their treatment in London. 'We had been fully prepared to meet all the costs involved in bringing them to the UK,' says Zafar Khan, the chairman of the Limbless Association. 'However, this wonderful gesture allows us to conserve some resources for the other Iraqi amputees.' Kuwait's Sheikh Sabah Al-Ahmad Al-Sabah also promised to rebuild the boys' homes in Iraq and to provide financially for their families.

When Nafisah heard that Ali would be leaving in less than

three weeks, she and Ali began to work even harder together. 'When I learned he would be going to London, I told Ali that I had to teach him as much as I could. He has a very strong will and he really, really wanted to learn whatever would help him,' she says. 'His intelligence will enable him to overcome his disability and lead a normal life, but so would learning some coping techniques.'

During the next three weeks Ali continued with the strengthening exercises that would enable him to support the new arms when he got them. He also practised opening the zipper on his bag and tried out different ways to carry a bag. 'I wanted him to be able to take responsibility for his possessions when he went to school,' says Nafisah, who tried to push all her love into the boy in the time remaining. When she took him on a final outing with her children and husband, Ali suddenly became silent and started to weep. Says Nafisah, 'He told me, "This reminds of my times with my father; I miss my parents."'

Two weeks before Ali was due to fly to the UK, his uncle Mohammed was flown back to Baghdad by military helicopter to see his family in Za'Faraniya. He took several large boxes of gifts that had been donated to Ali for the family. Mohammed hadn't seen his family for four months, and he found the short visit to his beloved family emotionally complicated. 'It was wonderful to see my family, but it was so hard to leave them by themselves again. I was also worried about Ali.' He says he tried to be strong at his departure, which was necessary in order to accompany Ali to the UK. The tears came when he landed back in Kuwait four days later. During his visit Mohammed had also met Ahmed's father, Mohammed Hamza, for the first time and had discussed details of the trip to England. They struck up an easy rapport over several cups of chai, which was good, because – like their boys – they would soon be offering each other a great deal of companionship in an unfamiliar land.

While Uncle Mohammed was away, Ahmed decided to keep

Ali company by sleeping in his room. During the vacuum of his uncle's absence, Ali had started dwelling on his lost family, and this led to some upsetting dreams about his beautiful mother, naughty little brother and charismatic father. 'When Uncle Mohammed went back to Iraq, I missed him a lot,' says Ali. 'I really wanted him to get there safely so that he could see his family. I also wanted to hear news of my sisters, but I was surprised by how much I missed him.' On Friday, the Muslim holy day, Nafisah was at home with her family when she received a phone call from Catherine Ecolivet. 'She told me how depressed and frustrated Ali had become since Mohammed had left a few days before,' says Nafisah, who decided the only thing for it would be to transport husband and children to Ali's bedside for the rest of the day in an attempt to cheer him up.

Ali also told her that he was feeling increasingly frustrated at the loss of his arms. He wasn't a baby, but he felt so dependent. 'I couldn't wait to get my arms so I could eat things like rice and soup by myself, and go to the toilet by myself as well,' he recalls. He wanted to be able to scratch his inflamed skin, to adjust the pressure garment when it chafed his neck, to wash his face again. But most of all, he yearned to hug his sisters.

PART THREE

England

CHAPTER SIXTEEN

A Red Tie and a White Shirt

'London is very beautiful. It is very green, the streets are nice and big, and the river Thames looks so nice and cool. It reminds me of the Diyala River where I used to fish. English children are lucky to live in such a wonderful and peaceful country. So many others are not in that position and are suffering, like my friends in Iraq. I want to return back to Iraq once I get treated. I want to go to school and become a translator, and drive my car up and down Baghdad streets. I am learning English and I want to work in a university as a translator.

'I am looking forward to going to a football match in England. Manchester United is the best team and David Beckham is my favourite player, but I am very cross that he has gone to Real Madrid. This is very bad.

'I don't blame the British people for what happened to me. The people of the US and the UK are really good and kind. It is their governments who did the bombing, not them. It is like Kuwait and Iraq. The Kuwaitis are my friends – they don't blame ordinary Iraqi people for Iraq's invasion of their country. I only wish my family could be safe here with me. It would be so nice for them to share the experience of living on the other side of the world.'

Ali Ismaeel Abbas

Like an airborne *Orient Express*, the prime minister of Kuwait's plane was an essay in opulence. The £30 million Gulfstream V is a very upmarket private jet that can carry up to 18 passengers in extreme luxury. Ali and Ahmed stared in disbelief at their dazzling new surroundings. The walls were lined in pale blue suede, with matching electric blinds. The seats, adorned with red carnations, looked more like luxurious armchairs – there was even a bed in a berth at the rear of the cabin where they were invited to sleep if they felt tired. The interior trim was made from bird's-eye maple varnished to a mirror-like shine, and in the on-board bathroom, where vases of fresh roses scented the air, were real gold taps. As the 30-metre-long jet reached its cruising altitude 16 kilometres above the dusty desert landscape, and headed north-west through Saudi airspace at nearly the speed of sound, glamorous air hostesses proffered platters of canapés. Soon a cocktail party atmosphere filled the cabin: Dr Al-Shatti from the Ministry of Health and Zafar Khan from the Limbless Association discussed Ali's future; Dr Al-Najada and Dr Sabreen appreciated the chance to put their feet up; in one corner the boys' guardians sipped fruit juice and peered out of the window; in another, Alexandra Williams, the *Daily Mirror* journalist, was interviewing Nafisah, Ali's physiotherapist, who had agreed to leave her children for a week in order to help Ali settle down in London. It was quite a gathering. The life of Ali Ismaeel Abbas had taken a new and exotic turn since Sheikh Al-Sabah had offered his private plane for the journey to England. A lot had happened in the past few days.

When Ali and Ahmed found out that they were going to be travelling to England together, they were very excited. But Ali was upset to be leaving the tender and supportive care of Nafisah, his physiotherapist. 'Nafisah, please come with me to England,' he said. 'I refuse to go unless you come too. Come for a few days at least.'

'Well, why not, Ali!' she replied with an indulgent smile. She only realized he was serious when she saw the look of relief and delight that transformed his face from misery to elation. 'Well, Ali, I don't know if this will be possible. It's not really up to me. I have my family to look after, and I can't just invite myself, you know.'

She might as well have waved a red rag at a bull. Over the next few days she marvelled at Ali's resolve as he asked Dr Al-Shatti and his doctors whether Nafisah could fly to London with him. He asked her husband and he asked her children. Fortunately they all said yes. Nafisah was to come to London for a week. 'I realized it would be good to meet his new physio-therapist and the occupational therapist, to give Ali some continuity of care,' she says. 'It was an upheaval, but you have to understand I would do anything for this boy.'

Dr Al-Shatti had recently returned from London where he had been helping the Limbless Association finesse the arrangements for Ali and Ahmed's arrival – bringing four non-English-speaking Iraqi citizens to a new life in the UK was a great responsibility for the small charity, and they wanted to get everything right. He showed the boys photographs of the large house near the hospital that the charity had rented for them. Backing on to a golf course, it has a mock-Tudor façade, a large garden with an apple tree, five bedrooms and a well-equipped kitchen. At the charity's request, one more bedroom with a spacious en suite bathroom was in the process of being carved from the downstairs space, with a view to allowing wide enough access for Ahmed's wheelchair.

Visas, allowing them to enter the UK for medical treatment, had also been arranged. Ali and Mohammed would be going, and so would Ahmed and the father he had not seen for more than four months. Five days before they flew to England, Ahmed was finally reunited with his father, Mohammed Hamza. It had been a long and painful separation. 'When I heard that my father was here, I pushed my wheelchair really fast into the lift and downstairs to see him,' says Ahmed, excitedly. Mohammed says it was the happiest moment of his life. 'For two months I had been unable to contact my children. We thought Ahmed was dead, and he thought we were dead.'

During the boys' last week in Kuwait they had gone to a party at a restaurant, where all the children at the hospital were entertained with music, dancing and fancy-dress cartoon characters. 'The last night we stayed in the hospital the nurses came and they brought their children,' remembers Ali. 'There were cameras and we took photos … they were crying, we were crying.'

Before they left Kuwait, Ali and Ahmed visited the new prime minister at his office to thank him personally for his country's assistance. Ali wore a crisp white shirt, grey trousers and a red tie bought for him by Mohammed Al-Bader, the air traffic controller. 'You can't imagine the effort I went to so that Ali could wear that red tie,' he says. 'Looking at Ali's face, I decided that a red tie would be perfect for him – but it took two weeks to find one. It is difficult to find a red tie with an elasticated neck in the right size during the summer season in Kuwait.'

Ali kissed the bespectacled Sheik on both cheeks in a traditional greeting, and spoke the words he had been preparing for the past two days. 'You never spared anything to help me,' said Ali confidently.

'We will provide everything you need – now don't use your new arms to hit others!' the premier told the boy with a smile. Ali issued a musical laugh, and told the attendant media that he really wanted to be able to drive a car, God willing.

Alexandra Williams's presence on the plane was explained by the Limbless Association's recent decision to accept a joint offer from the *Daily Mirror* and *Tonight With Trevor McDonald* to cover Ali's story, organised in an attempt to shield Ali from the huge media interest in him. When Alexandra had returned to

Kuwait on 5 August, two days before the flight to the UK, she was as impressed by the change in Ali as Andrea Catherwood had been in June. 'Physically Ali even looked different: his eyes didn't seem so large and he'd put on a bit of weight,' she remembers. 'I'd seen photographs, but it was amazing to actually see him in person. He was running all over the hospital, pushing Ahmed's wheelchair up and down the corridors at a furious rate. He used his teeth to dress and called a lift for me using his nose. His uncle told him that his nose would get flat from overuse! What the doctors had done for him was remarkable. They'd given him back his life.'

It was as if the child in Ali had come back. 'He was just so positive,' says Alexandra. 'I don't think he knows the meaning of self-pity. I asked Mohammed if Ali ever got depressed, and he had to scratch his head and think a bit to come up with a single instance.'

There were tearful scenes at the hospital as the nurses helped the boys pack their bags on the morning of their departure, 7 August. Ali thanked them all for looking after him. Some, he kissed. To others, he offered his right residual limb to shake goodbye. Mohammed Al-Jarralleh, Kuwait's minister of health, saw the boys to the airport. Inside the plane was Mohammed Al-Bader who had used his contacts at the airport to wangle the surprise goodbye. 'When he saw me waiting inside, he started yelling with excitement,' says the avuncular air traffic controller. 'I will never forget that moment. Each smile on Ali's face was a clear victory.'

Ali had been so excited about going to London that he had barely slept the previous night. 'I want new arms more than anything. I want to be normal again,' he told Alexandra on the flight, before bombarding her with questions about life in the UK, a country far removed from all that was familiar to him. 'He asked question after question about London,' recalls Alexandra fondly. 'He talked about David Beckham a lot, and was fascinated with girls' belly buttons – he wanted to know if mine was pierced.' She made up for his disappointment that it was not by informing him that some girls have their noses or tongues pierced. Ali screamed in delight when he heard that. 'He also found my clothes hilarious and asked me, "Do all girls show their arms and wear T-shirts that are too small?"'

Ali really liked this young woman with the long blonde hair. He thought she was funny, and he was keen to show off all his new skills. He asked her to put her laptop computer on the carpet so he could type with his toes, and then he decided to arm-wrestle her, with his right residual limb, which is surprisingly powerful. Next, he clasped her hairbrush under his chin and tried to brush her hair. She laughed when he picked up her glasses with his toes. He quickly grabbed her mobile phone and pretended to chat to his sisters. When it was time for lunch he refused to let Mohammed feed him. He picked up a fork between his toes and proudly ate a carrot by himself, smiling so much he could barely swallow.

As the plane touched down, Ali peered out of the windows and saw, to his amazement, that they had landed on a football pitch. There were the white lines, but where were the goalposts?

The confident little boy who emerged from the private jet at RAF Northolt a little after 3 p.m. on Thursday 7 August 2003 was unrecognizable from the burned child of a few months before. Smartly dressed, in his distinctive red tie and white shirt, he was smiling broadly, apparently unfazed by the TV crews on the tarmac. Britain was in the grip of a summer heat wave and the sky was a flawless Tiffany blue. He couldn't believe how hot it was. 'Can you take me to the football?' he demanded of reporters as he stepped on to British soil.

Among the small welcoming party bathed in the warm sunshine was Diana Morgan. For the past three months she and Zafar Khan had worked doggedly on Ali's behalf. Now she was about to meet the boy himself for the first time. 'I could sense that the two television cameras were trained on me, anticipating a tearful reaction, but I didn't cry and cry – I was just too happy,' she says. As Diana said, 'Hello Ali,' she noticed that he seemed quite shy. Then her attention was drawn to Ahmed as she wanted him to feel equally welcome. Soon she was sitting next to the boys, saying silly things like, 'David Beckham'. She didn't speak any Arabic, but she wanted them to feel as comfortable as possible.

The Kuwaiti embassy had sent a fleet of seven elegant Mercedes to collect the party. However, as these swept in majestic convoy through the front gates of the airbase, the party left discreetly from a side exit in a people-carrier with blacked-out windows. It was important that the location of Ali's new home was kept secret so he wasn't subjected to too much unwanted scrutiny.

Ali's first impression was that his new semi-detached house on an arterial road in south-west London was very strange indeed. It was tall, with a curious stripy black-and-white façade, and cars sped by, very fast, right outside. At the back was a private garden and inside was a revelation: stairs. It was more like the hospital in Kuwait than a house. There seemed to be walls everywhere and no way out. Ali ran up the final flight, wondering if he would emerge on the roof. Instead, he pushed open the door to the attic bedroom with his foot and ran to look out of the window at the garden far below. He felt so high up. In Baghdad his house had all been on the ground, but here you might fall out of a window if you weren't careful.

CHAPTER SEVENTEEN
A Gifted Limb-Maker

'When I first saw this house in London, I thought it was a very strange house indeed. It felt good to be in a house, out of a hospital, but it also seemed a bit odd at first because you either have to stay in the garden to play football or you are inside. Back at home I used to go with my friends to places about one kilometre from home: to the stream, to the Diyala River, and to collect shells. There were so many of us playing football, and we were surrounded by green stuff. We had a lot of freedom. But now I'm used to it, I really like it here.'

Ali Ismaeel Abbas

Ali booted the ball towards the net. Goal! Then he ran forward, rescued it with a deft clip of the toe, and dribbled it back towards Ahmed who was lying on the grass. Taking careful aim, he kicked it gently towards his friend: he wanted him to feel fully included in the game. Ahmed, propped up on his arms, headed the bouncing ball with enthusiasm. Ali couldn't believe that there were goalposts in his own garden. The lush green grass looked just like the football pitches he had seen on television – he pretended he was David Beckham.

Ali had picked a bedroom next to Uncle Mohammed's, and

had unpacked his family photos and the hundreds of letters he'd received in Kuwait. They'd had a *halal* Indian takeaway the night they arrived – Ali had felt quite upset when several of his guests started drinking beer, something he'd never witnessed before. They played football most of Friday, as well as an electronic ice hockey game they'd been given. Ali punched the controls with his toes, while Ahmed used his left hand. They'd also been visited by Andrea Catherwood, who'd brought her adorable black Labrador puppy to visit.

It was now Saturday morning and the *Daily Mirror* had hired a red double-decker bus to show Ali and Ahmed the best bits of their adoptive city. But first, Ali had to hide Diana's stick one more time (she had told him that both her legs were prosthetic limbs). Although he could tell she had a good sense of humour, when he stole her stick this time she did something he could barely believe – she got up and walked across the room towards him shrieking with laughter. Diana was always laughing, but now she was walking without her stick as well. 'At that moment I think Ali began to realize just what it was possible for a double amputee to achieve,' muses Diana.

Thomas Edwards, the burger van man who had sent the clothes and the video to Kuwait, was there and so was Diana's beautiful 10-year-old, Lara, at whom Ali smiled shyly. As the bus moved along in the sunshine, he ran up and down the top deck, affectionately nudging Nafisah and Dr Sabreen with the top of his head. At Buckingham Palace Ali declared, 'It's a palace big enough for two queens,' and told the reporters gravely that no-one was allowed near Saddam's palaces: 'there was a risk of being shot and killed'. The bus continued onwards towards Piccadilly Circus and Trafalgar Square, where Ali looked up at Lord Nelson on his column and asked, 'Who is he? And how did he lose his arm?'

At Regent's Park Zoo Ali stroked the soft fur of a racoon with his feet. The bus then stopped for an ice cream next to the biggest clock they had ever seen, which overlooked a wide river that reminded him of the Diyala. Finally, they went to a toy shop at least as big as Ibn Sina Hospital.

But on Sunday Ali couldn't stop concerns about the following day crowding into his head. At last he would be meeting the doctors who would be responsible for giving him new arms, but he was worried: what if they took one look at him and shook their heads? What if there was some problem with his amputations? Ali was tired, but barely slept that night. When he awoke he felt even more apprehensive. 'I was worried the doctor would ask where my parents are and I'd have to tell him,' he told Alexandra Williams quietly.

Twenty-four technicians in white aprons stand at well-used wooden benches creating custom-made body parts. Each artificial limb built at Queen Mary's is a one-off, a small work of art patiently assembled by hand inside the hangar-like workshop where the sounds of chiselling, sawing, hammering and grinding fill the air.

Some of the technicians are patiently building up leg or foot forms from pools of molten wax or shaping pieces of carbon fibre. Others tear open bags of dusty dental plaster to make plaster casts of shoulders or calves. There are tubs of liquid silicone, offcuts of leather, bales of skin-coloured foam rubber and sheets of shiny aluminium. Ancient Singer sewing machines are available for anyone who needs to sew on a Velcro tab or make a strap to hold a new limb in position.

Metal shelving carries intriguing labels: 'New Sockets', 'Limbs for Finishing', 'Limbs for Trial'. There are boxes of hands and legs in progress, and some finished limbs are propped up against some of the work benches. One slender right leg wears a stocking and a gold velvet evening shoe. Another much bigger leg is dressed in gentleman's black brogues, and a third is already impressively equipped with a gleaming trainer and sport sock.

Photographs taken at Queen Mary's after the First World War reveal that this workshop and its wooden benches have remained virtually unchanged since the early twentieth century. However, although limb technology itself may not yet offer the sci-fi bionic vision of the *Terminator* films, it has evolved considerably in the thirty years: the development of substances like silicone and carbon-fibre mean limbs are lighter and stronger than ever before.

At one end of the workshop is a display of funky-patterned limbs in zebra-style black and white, Jackson Pollock-inspired spattered red and orange – even a paisley blue-and-white number. 'Some people like to show off their new legs and arms and therefore ask us to make something a bit different. They might have sensible day-to-day limbs, but want a more light-hearted pair for doing sport,' says Nick Hillsdon, a senior prosthetist at RSL Steeper, the prosthetic limb manufacturing company that has been based at the hospital since 1921. Steeper was founded to serve the needs of the limbless veterans of the First World War. Under contract to the NHS, it employs the prosthetists and technicians who form an integral part of the multidisciplinary team that care for patients like Ali and Ahmed, and, crucially, it is the only British company that manufactures prosthetic arms. Steeper has also been working with the Kuwaiti Ministry of Health for many years.

Nick Hillsdon is Britain's leading upper-limb specialist. Since the mid-1970s, this tall and broad, yet quietly spoken, medical engineer has helped many hundreds of people lead active lives with new custom-built arms from the Steeper workshops. Many of his patients are children when he first meets them, and he particularly enjoys watching them develop into independent adults. But before Ali could meet this gifted limb-maker in one of a maze of fitting rooms near the fascinating workshop, he first had to meet the consultant in a nearby office who would examine him prior to treatment: would the consultant take one look at Ali's injuries and shake his head?

Dr Sellaiah Sooriakumaran trained in Sri Lanka before undertaking postgraduate study in prosthetic surgery and rehabilitation in the UK. In 1990 he was appointed Consultant in Rehabilitation Medicine at Queen Mary's, where he prefers to introduce himself to new patients simply as Dr Soori. There is little in the prosthetics field that he and his team of therapists and prosthetists have not seen. He relishes being able to help patients with complex physical problems, and enjoys learning from them.

It is much more common to survive the loss of a leg than an arm. Figures suggest that for every 20 people who receive a prosthetic lower limb, just one person will receive a new arm. When someone loses both arms at such a high point – in Ali's case, almost to the shoulder – they also usually lose their sight at best (due to the face's close proximity to the trauma site), or their life at worst. For Ali's lovely face to have survived entirely unscathed when in such close proximity to his ruined arms is extremely unusual.

'Bomb blasts are generally the only thing that causes injuries exactly like Ali's,' explains Dr Soori. 'Children sometimes lose their hands or their fingers because of septicaemia or gangrene. Several years ago a number lost a single arm or hand to meningitis, but it is rare to lose both arms, particularly above the elbow.' They may be unusual, but those patients in a similar circumstance to Ali have gone on to lead genuinely independent lives: they drive cars, work, get married, have children and, in one case, have learned to fly a plane. Dr Soori recognized that a positive attitude has a great deal to do with what amputees can go on to achieve, but so does the length of the residual limb – too short and it might not be possible to fit artificial arms.

Dr Soori had followed Ali's story and felt the responsibility of being the clinician ultimately responsible for returning him to independence. He knew that the young boy about to appear in his office for his initial appointment was a rare case. He also nursed some anxieties about what he would find, and expected Ali to be severely traumatized by his ordeal. 'I'd seen the news and I knew the extent of the scarring and burns,' he says. 'I imagined a child who would be psychologically severely affected and probably in pain ... and then here he was!'

Ali's moment of judgement arrived a few minutes after 11 a.m. on Monday 11 August. Ali said hello to Dr Soori's secretary, Debbie, and then walked into the adjacent office with Diana and Mohammed. Dr Soori gave a cheery greeting, but behind his warm smile he was observing the boy with a clinician's detachment – looking for important clues to his emotional state. He was immediately impressed. Ali made eye contact readily. He did not seem frightened to expose his amputations to scrutiny. He seemed intelligent, alert and eager to learn, if a little taciturn. Abdu Haider, a Lebanese-born prosthetist who works for RSL Steeper, was also in the room and he was able to act as interpreter between Dr Soori and Ali. After examining Ali closely, the doctor was able to explain that he felt certain there was adequate muscle and soft tissue cover over the bone of his longer right arm to allow operation of the myo-electric hand. When Abdu Haider explained that the doctor said he would be able to have new arms, Ali was ecstatic. He started asking questions. He didn't want to waste any time now.

'I thought he had coped tremendously well,' says Dr Soori. 'He presented as a normal kid who wanted to get right on with treatment, and this certainly made my job easier. We often find ourselves learning from the positivity of children like this.' Dr Soori had expected to refer the boy to a psychiatrist, but found this unnecessary. He sensed that the support Ali had been receiving from his family and his new friends, as well as from the international attention focused on his situation, had proved very effective in his psychological recovery. 'Somehow he had managed to find a way to turn his circumstances to his advantage, which is amazing when you consider the trauma and multiple bereavements he has suffered.'

A lively hospital press conference followed Ali's consultation. The journalists were told that both Ali and Ahmed would be fitted with the limbs within a few weeks, but that it would be up to six months before they could use them proficiently. Their programme of treatment would involve taking detailed measurements and castings of the boys' residual limbs, the manufacture of replacements, and an intensive rehabilitative programme. This would include physiotherapy sessions to increase their flexibility, and OT (occupational therapy) to teach them how to use the new arms. The journalists were told that both boys, until fully grown, would require new limbs every few years and, thereafter, the limbs would need replacing approximately every four years, due to wear and tear.

The following day Dr Soori wrote to Greg Williams, the Consultant Burns Surgeon at Chelsea and Westminster Hospital in London's Fulham Road, who would be responsible for monitoring Ali's skin grafts.

Ali is a previously healthy boy who sustained 35 per cent deep burns affecting both upper limbs, anterior trunk, and flanks. Following a stormy period of management he had both upper limbs amputated, the left side at through shoulder level with about 2–3cm humeral bone remnant and the right side at mid-humeral level. The lower limbs are spared and following several skin grafts, harvested from the back and posterior aspect of the thighs, the plastic surgeons in Kuwait have managed to achieve full healing. Fortunately, the right dominant residual upper limb is of adequate length and has good soft tissue cover. Unfortunately, the left shoulder [residual limb] is covered with grafted skin and would warrant special material on the socket of the prosthesis to avoid skin breakdown. From a general medical point of view he has recovered fully and is currently on no medications. Dr Al-Najada will be accompanying Ali to discuss the past plastic surgical management.

Small specks of dripping plaster splashed on to the floor. Nick Hillsdon reached for another strip of the plaster-soaked bandage, dipped it in warm water and shaped it over Ali's shoulder. It was a bit like making papier mâché. It was 18 August and Ali was having his first casting for his new right arm. Slowly the plaster dried out, and as it did so, it hardened. Soon Nick was able to slide it off. A perfect jelly-mould of Ali's residual limb, which together with the measurements Nick had taken would allow him to construct a snug-fitting socket for the replacement limb. Attached to this would be Ali's new right arm. 'His right shoulder is a nice mobile shoulder with a good-length residual limb. He should be able to activate a hand and elbow quite well,' Nick told Mohammed after examining Ali.

Nick Hillsdon privately recognized, however, that he faced a considerable challenge to give Ali the state-of-the-art mechanical replacement arm he craved. Ali needed not just a hand, but a wrist and an elbow as well. Each of these elements had to be easily operable: Nick had to devise the mechanical means by which Ali could flex the elbow, twist the wrist and open and close the fingers of the hand. 'This was a first for us,' says Nick. 'We've never built an arm with a wrist rotator, a "flexion-assist" elbow and an electric hand. We've supplied each element individually, many times, but putting them all together in one arm was new ground for us.' Such a complex approach was considered the best option because Ali had lost both arms. 'We probably wouldn't have given all that to him if he'd lost just one arm, but we wanted Ali to have as much functionality as possible.' In cases where one real arm remains, patients generally come to rely on it – a prosthetic arm or hand is no substitute for the real thing. A cosmetic arm or one with limited function is therefore usually sufficient.

Yet Nick's solution for Ali couldn't be too heavy or too difficult to operate. Ali needed to be able to wear his £12,000 electric arm, a gift from the Kuwaiti government, with ease. A good fit was particularly important: if the socket that supported the arm moved around at all, it was likely to abrade the fragile skin at the site of the amputation. Furthermore, Nick intended to fit small electrodes inside the socket that would allow Ali to control the fingers on his bionic hand. These would press against Ali's skin and respond to the electrical impulses from his muscles, triggering an electronic switch that would allow him to open and close his fingers at will. If the socket shifted position, however, the contact would be lost and the fingers would remain frozen, however much he signalled his desire to open the hand.

Not only would training be required to learn to control its ferocious grip; Ali would also have to master the mechanical elbow. This is controlled by swinging the arm forward, flicking it up and locking it in position by rapidly rotating his right shoulder. There was also the new bionic wrist to learn to use. This is operated by a strap across his chest; pulling the shoulders back activates an electric motor in the wrist: a strong tug and the wrist rotates clockwise; a weak tug and it rotates anticlockwise. After training and practice, these movements would eventually be subconsciously assimilated – just like riding a bike or driving a car.

Mastering all of this in just one arm would be challenging enough, so Nick decided that Ali's left replacement arm would be a lightweight, non-functioning cosmetic prosthetic to start with. Costing around £7000, it would be designed to look as natural as possible. And although it would not contain any electronics, it would allow Ali to support objects. Most importantly, it would give him the gift of normality: two arms where they should be. Ali Abbas would once again look like everyone else.

Two weeks later, on 27 August, Ali returned to the prosthetist whom he and Ahmed had now nicknamed 'Jean-Claude van Damme'. The trial socket was ready. Inside the pale brown plastic was an electrode attached to wires that connected with a bionic hand. Nick told Ali to tense the muscle he used to move his residual limb towards his rib cage, but after repeated attempts the fingers refused to respond. 'I'm sorry, Ali. The position of the electrode isn't quite right,' Nick said, his words translated by Zena Al-Ugaily, an Iraqi woman who was flown to the UK in December 2000 to receive a prosthetic limb after she had lost her left leg in a road traffic accident in Abu Dhabi. 'We have to expect a bit of trial and error,' he explained, as he headed back to the drawing board to make another socket. Ali was disappointed, but only had to wait another week.

Ali hoped he'd be able to make the fingers work this time. He'd been running through in his head what he had to do: push the residual limb against the side of his body – and the hand opens; do it again – and the hand closes. That was the theory anyway.

Initially, Ali found the hand difficult to operate. 'I can feel him moving them. They are moving slightly on my hand,' said Nick, holding the fingers of the electric hand on his palm. But they refused to budge. Focusing intently on the fingertips of his new right hand Ali concentrated hard: a tiny movement. He gritted his teeth and tried again: suddenly, the fingers opened wide. He had worked the hand for the first time! This opened up all sorts of possibilities. He broke into a captivating smile. 'That moment was the happiest and most excited we'd ever seen Ali,' remembers Diana Morgan. 'He started cracking jokes and laughing.' Perhaps recalling Zafar's memorable introduction to the bionic hand all those months before in Kuwait, he had also hatched a plan. 'I want to pinch her nose,' he said in Arabic, grinning guilelessly at Alexandra Williams: 'Oh Alex, can you come here?'

'Don't go anywhere near it,' said Nick quickly. Alexandra extended her hand instead. 'All I can say is that I'm glad I didn't put my nose anywhere near that thing,' she says. Ali's new grip was ferocious: 'He'd cottoned on to the fact he had a lot of power.'

'The moment that Ali operated the hand was a break-through,' says Nick. 'Getting the control sites organized is the hardest thing, so we knew then he'd be all right.' Mohammed was also feeling more positive. Each time he and Ali went up to the hospital they saw other limbless people walking, eating, working and laughing – not least in the busy office of the Limbless Association where everyone just carries on as normal. 'Meeting other amputees living a normal life lifted our spirits so much,' insists Mohammed. 'I began to believe that one day Ali would be able to integrate fully. It was heart-warming for us to see everyone else coping so well.'

Fortunately, Ali Abbas was old enough to realize that his prosthetic limbs would not be real replacements. Young children sometimes imagine that the promise of a new arm or leg means their own will actually grow back, or that they will be given a new one by doctors that has all the fleshiness of the one they have lost or been born without. Igor Pavlovets, one of the first of a generation of children to be born with genetic deformities following the Chernobyl disaster, believed keenly that the left arm he had been promised to take the place of the limb he was denied by radiation poisoning would be as real as his existing powerful right arm. He was only six years old when he was told he would be coming to England from Belarus (in the former

Soviet Union) to receive the arm with which he wished to wash behind his ears. He would search the bags of foreign visitors to his orphanage in Minsk, hunting for his new limb. When Igor finally received his bionic arm in July 1994, from the same team working with Ali Abbas, it felt like something of a let-down – it wasn't real after all.

Twelve-year-old Ali was mature enough to have more realistic expectations and not to expect arms exactly like the ones he had lost. He also knew they were his only hope of future independence. It is difficult to imagine living without arms. We do so much with them that it is easy to take them for granted. But since the explosion, Ali had been unable to feed himself, comb his hair or clean his teeth; nor could he use the bathroom by himself or wash. His new arms would be tools of liberation, once again placing quite literally within his reach the thousands of daily tasks we take for granted. They would allow Ali to answer the phone, scratch an itch or blow his nose. In the future they would even allow him to drive a car. But first of all he would have to master them, a process that would take many, many months.

Thirteen-year-old Callum Heffy had never met Ali Abbas, but had heard about him on the news and knew that his father's friend, Nick Hillsdon, was helping to make his new arms. 'Callum, you are about the same height as Ali,' Nick explained. 'There are various formulae I can use for working out the correct length for Ali's new arms, but I always think it's better to find someone about the same size.' Callum kept very still as Nick measured his arms with a tape measure. He felt proud to be able to contribute in this small way.

While Nick got on with the process of ordering all the different components for Ali's new bionic arm, Ali tried to be patient. This was an act of will made more difficult by the fact that Ahmed had already been fitted with his new leg and was now walking short distances. He had also received a new electric hand. 'Nick, you keep making casts and taking measurements; when are you going to give me the arms?' Ali asked persistently.

'We're working as hard as we can Ali,' said the prosthetist gently. 'I understand how you feel, but your arm is a lot more complicated to manufacture than Ahmed's leg and hand.' It would also take Ali longer to learn to use it. Rehabilitation takes much longer for upper limb patients who rely on their arms for so many more tasks than walking or standing. Ali felt cross, frustrated and miserable. Each week of waiting felt like a month. Fortunately, several pleasant things were about to happen that would help distract him.

Very few people have survived injuries like those of Ali Abbas. While many patients treated at Roehampton have lost one or both hands, or perhaps an entire arm, very few people have 'high-level doubles' – where both hands as well as both elbows have been amputated. While it had been quietly inspiring for Ali to see leg amputees like Zafar and Diana succeeding in their lives, they knew it would be inspiring to introduce him to someone with similar disabilities who was nonetheless living a full and independent life. 'Being able to talk to someone with the same injuries definitely gives you hope,' says Diana. 'When I lost both my legs, I thought I was alone. Everyone else seemed to have lost just one leg.' A defining moment in her rehabilitation was being introduced to a jolly 22-year-old soldier who had also lost both legs, after stepping on a landmine. 'He came bounding into my hospital room, smiling and laughing. He was handsome and full of life. I asked him what difficulties he had, and he said none – except for when he got drunk. He said it made walking a bit more tricky! I was feeling rather low at the time, but he made me laugh a lot, and the minute he was there in front of me, wearing prosthetic legs and walking, I just knew I was going to be OK.'

Such meetings between volunteer and new amputees are at the core of the work carried out by the Limbless Association; but meeting Ali would be the first time Chris Garwood, 50, would be called upon to help in this way. The university lecturer had lost both his arms above the elbow when he was electrocuted on a railway line at the age of seven. Very few people with similar injuries survive.

Chris grew up in Barrow-in-Furness, Cumbria, before moving to London, but since 1977 has lived a fully independent life near Bologna, Italy, where he teaches simultaneous translation at universities there. He uses his arms to eat, drink and operate his computer. He can cook, dress and wash himself. He has fine motor control over his replacement hands and arms, and uses his hyper-mobile feet and toes – which have become very sensitive to touch – for an array of other tasks: removing floppy disks from his computer, opening drawers and doors, and deftly picking things up. 'It's almost as if I don't see myself as disabled and so others don't either,' he explains. 'Most things I can't do with my hands I can do easily with my feet. Not being able to hold hands with a girl is one of the big things I miss. Otherwise, I don't think that there are many things that I can't do.

'I remember one afternoon when I was about 16, thinking, "Why me?" I cried for about three hours. Then this nurse took me in to see this baby that had no legs, no arms, no ears, no eyes. I realized then that all you have to do is look around and you see people who are far worse off than you are.'

Chris is also one of Nick Hillsdon's patients – the prosthetist had decided to base the design of Ali's arms on those worn by Chris. The only difference is that Chris uses split hooks instead of electric hands; two neat hooks, designed to mimic the opposing action of thumb and forefinger, meet in a powerful grip. Prosthetic hands weren't available until the 1960s, and now Chris prefers hooks – partly because he is used to them, but also because they also allow very precise control. 'Probably a split hook would work better functionally for Ali, but for a young boy an electric hand is more cosmetically and socially acceptable,' explains Nick Hillsdon.

Ali and Chris met on 12 September at the Limbless Association's Gala Awards Dinner Presentation at a hotel in Kensington, west London. Ali won the Child of Inspiration Award and delighted everyone present by saying 'Thank you' in English, but he couldn't take his eyes off this man with the wide smile, aura of confidence and unusual hook-like hands. He watched impressed as Chris deftly picked up a glass of red wine, paused mid-anecdote, and took a refreshing sip. As Chris bent his elbow, Ali heard a hiss from a gas canister – although modern arms are now controlled by lithium ion battery, Chris had opted to retain the gas-powered technology with which he was also familiar. While Ali was fed mouthfuls of warm Mediterranean salad and sesame-topped salmon by Mohammed, he kept an eye on the table where Chris was eating these things by himself. He watched, mesmerized, as Chris deftly manipulated a spoon and demolished his sticky toffee pudding. His dexterity was inspiring enough, but it also looked as if Chris didn't even have to think much about what he was doing. He had assimilated his skills to the point where using his arms had become an unconscious process. 'Chris has become much bigger than his disability,' explains Diana. 'Even in a potentially difficult social scenario his personality is what engages you. It takes a long time and a great deal of practice to get to this automatic stage.'

Chris liked this bright-eyed boy with the camel-like lashes. 'I was amazed by how lively and happy he was,' he says. 'He reminded me of how the period immediately after I'd lost my arms was, ironically, one of the happiest of my life. Once I'd overcome the trauma, I was surrounded by fantastic people, I was fed by nurses, I always had company, I had a great teacher and I got a much better education than I would otherwise have had. Reality struck only when I got my arms and tried starting to do things on my own. That's the hardest challenge and learning how to do things for yourself is a very slow process,' says Chris who has now had four decades of experience since he was fitted with his gas-operated replacements.

Chris gently cautioned Ali about expecting too much too soon. 'To be honest, it takes years to learn how to use prosthetic arms well. You get the basics after a few months, but it takes far longer to do anything with any degree of ease. The instructors can only indicate certain things, so you have to invent a lot for yourself.'

As a child Chris had been used to drinking by picking up a glass with his teeth; and he wrote with his mouth; but as he grew older these particular coping skills became less appropriate. 'Landlords would tick me off for playing around by drinking my beer without using my hands; it became uncomfortable signing cheques at the bank with my mouth,' he says. 'I wanted to fit in socially, so I had to start again with a lot of things.'

They were grateful for his measured comments, but just seeing Chris living such an independent life gave Ali and Mohammed real hope. 'From that point Ali started to believe that if he continues to work, anything would be possible,' says Mohammed.

It was an England shirt printed with the magic number seven: the number of David Beckham, his hero. He could hardly believe that he, Ali Ismaeel Abbas, was wearing it on the clipped turf in one of the world's most famous football stadiums. He looked up at thousands of empty seats that seemed to stretch all the way up to the clouds at Chelsea's Stamford Bridge, and imagined them full of roaring spectators. He was here at the west London stadium to help launch a campaign by CARE International to encourage soccer fans to donate a million shirts for Iraqi players and raise cash for the nation's impoverished children. 'Hello,

Ali. Do you like football?' asked England manager, Sven-Goran Eriksson. This was too much. 'Can you teach me to be as good as David Beckham?' said Ali. 'Let's play!' He and Ahmed got in some shooting practice with Sven, but the highlight came when the boys met several Iraqi footballers who had fled their country and now play for a Sunday league team in Fulham. Sadiq Al-Wohali, Abbas Aziz and their compatriots crowded around the boys, and together they chattered away in Arabic. 'I feel good around my own people,' said Ali. 'I want to be like my brothers. I am very happy to be in England getting treatment, but I miss my family and friends and people. This reminds me of Iraq and my surviving relatives.' He suddenly felt terribly home-sick. The following day, he was the subject of another *Daily Mirror* editorial: 'Six months ago Ali Abbas lay near death after his Iraq home was hit by a stray bomb. Yesterday he played football with England manager Sven-Goran Eriksson. That says a lot about the brilliant doctors who nursed him back to health. And even more about his indomitable spirit.'

'Meeting the Iraqi footballers was a powerful moment for Ali,' recalls Diana Morgan. 'It was wonderful for him to have such a warm welcome from his fellow Iraqis, but they also reminded him of everything he had left behind.' Ali had found a real fan in Diana: at a Limbless Association charity fun run in Richmond Park in late September she let him drive her scooter buggy as 37 amputees and wheelchair users joined a crowd of more than 300 other runners pounding around the course. 'Ali set off on his own on my buggy, which he loves, but which is of course adapted to hand controls only. He used his feet to steer and brake. He went a very long way and we had to keep calling to him to come back!'

As Ali hurtled off into the distance, Diana empathized with his excitement at such liberation. 'I vividly recall the first time I drove an adapted car after my accident,' she says. 'I cried all the way because I was finally moving quickly on my own without any assistance. It was the first time I had exerted my independence in over six months.' For Ali, being in control of something with wheels was not only exhilarating – it reminded him of driving his father's car through the muddy field in Za'Faraniya.

Since a few weeks after their arrival in London, several times a week Ali and Ahmed were driven to Queen Mary's, just 10 minutes away from their temporary home, for rehabilitation sessions. These would prepare the boys for their new limbs, and teach them how to use them, once delivered. Their occupational therapist, Fiona Carnegie, has a rich silky voice, a quick wit, boundless energy and lots of experience in dealing with children of all temperaments. She adopts a fair but firm approach, and has a strong desire to help her patients to become as independent as possible as quickly as possible, especially the double amputees. She observed immediately that Ali was intelligent and feisty, but more reflective and less outgoing than Ahmed.

In the early sessions Fiona helped Ali to learn techniques to use his feet for many of the tasks of daily living that he used to take for granted – the most hi-tech arms in the world can never be a substitute for real limbs. Fiona's strategy was to empower Ali to be able to use his feet with ease, giving him a range of choices in the future. It was a similar philosophy to that of Nafisah, the physiotherapist who had done so much for him in Kuwait and with whom Fiona had discussed Ali's case before she returned home to Kuwait in mid August, after her week in England.

During Ali's initial assessment on 21 August Fiona noted that he was able to use his feet to undress, write and eat. A week later she offered him a new challenge: Ali loved Coca-Cola, could he open a tab-can by himself? Sitting on a soft mat and concentrating hard, and after a few failed attempts, Ali succeeded in levering up the tab by holding an angled teaspoon between his toes. His reward, the mouth-watering hiss of escaping gas and the refreshing feel of the cool liquid sucked up through a straw. Soon he was filling the kettle with his feet, opening a jar of coffee with his toes, stirring sugar into a cup and, finally, with Fiona's assistance, pouring in the boiling water. And, when he thought she wasn't looking, he would hoover up coffee granules with his lips. A few days later he had learned to open a locked door by standing on one leg and turning a key with his toes.

'You play games and discover things at the same time,' explains Fiona, who has worked as an occupational therapist at Queen Mary's since 1981, helping her patients to achieve their goals by responding to their individual needs. 'I really enjoy watching limb-deficient children growing into together, OK adults.' Her approach to rehabilitation is an intuitive, often sub-conscious synthesis of ideas, rather than some inflexible text-book-based approach. 'Ideas for working with patients often come to me when I'm doing something completely different, like gardening or riding a bike,' she says, still rather surprised by her own instinctive approach.

Sometimes Ali's physiotherapists Penny Buttonshaw and Maggie Brennan took him to the famous Walking School and gym opened at Queen Mary's in February 1993 by Diana, Princess of Wales. 'Ali has brilliant balance; he can walk along a beam without any difficulty,' says Fiona who always works closely with the team of physios. Soon Ali was ready to try the treadmill. 'When he first started, we had to hold on to him while he was walking, but soon he was beginning to run,' says Penny. 'You can't imagine how brave that is.'

On 17 September, the day after he played football at Chelsea, Ali went swimming for the first time. He felt vulnerable and uncertain in the pool at Putney Hospital's neurodisability unit. He'd once been a fine river swimmer, but now felt apprehensive without arms to steady himself. Fiona held his head and encouraged him to lift his feet off the floor of the pool as he lay on his back. 'He did that OK, but when I said, "Now put your feet down," he panicked a bit and shouted, "I want to stop! I want to stop!"' she recalls. It was only when Fiona tried floating on her back herself, with her arms folded across her chest, and attempted to put her feet on the bottom of the pool that she realized just how difficult it was to move underwater without arms. At the next swimming session Ali was determined to rediscover his old confidence. With Fiona's help he chose an inflated horse-shoe shaped buoyancy aid, and manoeuvred it under his right residual limb and around his neck. This time he would face forward. He pushed off with his feet and had soon begun to swim. 'Yes, Ali, yes. You're doing it; you're swimming, Ali,' urged Penny sitting on the edge of the pool ahead of him as Fiona walked beside the ecstatic, swimming boy. 'Swimming is a very big deal for an amputee,' explains Diana Morgan, who well remembers swimming for the first time – in the same pool with the same physios – after her accident. 'You think it's going to be horrible to have to expose your body, but the freedom of weightlessness just takes you over.'

Ali tried to wait patiently for the new arms, and he watched enviously as Ahmed practised walking on his new lower leg. Ali was also refining his new skills: playing Game Boy with his feet, unwrapping a Kit Kat with his toes – even partially dressing himself by using his feet to push a T-shirt over his head as Fiona had shown him. He also loved to play with the Iraqi children who came to visit. He was particularly fond of Faisel, the five-year-old son of Zena Al-Ugaily, the Arabic interpreter. Ali would lie on the carpet, tickling Faisel with his toes while the younger child squealed with laughter. With Zena's help the Limbless Association had recently engaged a young Iraqi private maths tutor in her early twenties to teach the boys English. Zainab Hashim taught at the house in the early evenings, four or five times a week. 'When I saw Ali on television in hospital in Iraq I'd cried my eyes out,' she says. 'I used to wonder what I could do to help, so it was amazing when I was asked to teach them English. It was also a challenge – they are very lively boys who like to tease me a lot.' Zainab's father runs a grocery specializing in Middle Eastern food, so in the early days she would often arrive with bags of familiar ingredients that Uncle Mohammed would cook up into fragrantly scented dishes of grilled lamb and chicken, cooked with tomato, garlic, onion and chickpeas, and accompanied by rice, flat bread and palate-cleansing chunks of salted cucumber.

Ali was reluctant to start lessons at first, and both boys seemed a bit bored, so Zainab took them on outings to the cinema and to visit her friends who lived nearby. She worked hard to make the lessons fun, though she discovered that she had to offer incentives. 'Ali would pester me to go for a spin in the car, or to eat a *shawarma* (a Middle Eastern savoury) and would promise to study really hard in return,' she says, laughing. Ali displayed a natural facility for English and responded well to this engaging young woman with her cheerful sense of humour, who found it quite a challenge to keep control of her exuberant charges. 'I didn't want them to dread me coming to teach them,' she says, explaining that because of the trauma Ali had been through, she felt quite unable to treat him strictly. 'I do love this boy to bits. He doesn't have a lot of women in his life, and so I quickly became like a sister. Ali picked up English very quickly – often he would say something in Arabic and ask me to interpret it into English, and then he'd spend the next few days saying, "I can't be bothered," or some such! And although he is shy about talking to other people, he could soon understand a huge amount of English.' It was when Zainab encouraged him to make phone calls that the extent of his learning really emerged. He would tuck the phone into his shoulder, under his chin, and chat away to Diana in well-structured flurries of good English, asking lots of questions and cracking jokes.

* * *

On 29 September 2003 Ali's bionic right arm was ready for the final fitting. All the mechanical elements – socket, elbow, wrist and hand – had now been fashioned into a perfect, pale brown whole. Ali returned as usual to treatment room six, at the end of a short carpeted corridor. Inside, everything looked the same as before – same old dripping tap and leaking Belfast sink, same old Bob the Builder and Pooh posters stuck to the walls. But today everything felt different. 'I was very eager to see the arm, and when I did I was overjoyed,' says Ali. 'It was very much what I had in my mind, having seen the one that Zafar brought to Kuwait.'

Nick slid the arm's socket on to Ali's shoulder and attached it, with Fiona's help, with temporary straps so that Ali could wear it unsupported for the first time. He wouldn't receive the cosmetic left arm for another week, and the two were designed to be worn together.

The arm felt heavy. It weighed 1.5 kilograms – approximately the same weight as the right arm he had lost, yet felt heavier as it was self-supported by muscles and tendons within. 'I just thought, "I've got to get used to it; I have to,"' recalls Ali. 'I was very eager to start practising. When I finally got to put the arm on, Ahmed peeled an orange for me and I used my artificial arm to eat it. I was so happy!' Uncle Mohammed says it was only at that moment, however, that Ali fully realized that the prosthetic arms would never be able to compensate for his missing limbs. 'He had hoped he would be able to use the arms for doing plenty of things, principally washing and going to the toilet; and although they brought him hope, he realized he had to dramatically scale down his expectations.'

Learning to operate the arm was to prove much harder than he had imagined.

CHAPTER EIGHTEEN

'I'm All Here now'

'I used to like school, but they used to hit us a lot. Once, in Iraq, a lady teacher had hit a pupil. I said "Why did you do that?" so she hit me too. Then when all the class, including me, failed a test, the teacher hit us all with a stick. After that, I learned everything and never got hit again.

'My favourite subject is geography. I like it a lot. I used to like learning about which country had oil, which was best for agriculture, that sort of thing. There's another subject I enjoyed: agriculture. I used to get higher marks, but I didn't like it as much.

'My primary school in Iraq is called Salam, which means "peace". It was a very big school with about 1000 students. There were 40 in my class. It was two kilometres from my home. Sometimes we walked; sometimes we used a car. I was six when I went to that school.

'My school in England is better than in Baghdad. Sometimes we play in the headmaster's office. In Baghdad if we did that, he would kill us. I once saw my friend hitting the headmaster. If someone at my school in Iraq did that, he would get beaten up by the headmaster all year long.'

Ali Ismaeel Abbas

Tim Hobbs started his unconventional school in 1990 in a church hall in Wimbledon, south-west London, with just nine pupils. He was teaching at a famous London preparatory school at the time and could see that his tutor group felt stifled and unhappy by the school's old-fashioned approach. 'They weren't allowed to talk at lunch, and all their learning was classroom based. I wanted to remedy all the things that were troubling them,' says this charismatic and energetic innovator. Soon the children were climbing trees, learning by exploring outside the classroom, and challenging their creativity. It was an inventive approach that was soon producing exceptionally well-rounded children as well as good academic results. In 1998 John Clare, *The Daily Telegraph*'s Education Editor, picked Hall School as one of the country's most outstanding independent day schools, and described it as an 'unusual, delightful, fast-developing school'. Now, at two sites, it has 650 pupils of all nationalities and abilities.

Tim Hobbs believes in developing children's sense of self-worth, so when he had read in the newspaper that Ali and Ahmed would be coming to London for treatment at Queen Mary's, he thought they might like to join his friendly school between treatments. 'We take children to Queen Mary's sometimes, and I thought Ali and Ahmed might get a bit bored being there all the time,' he explains. In early September he wrote a letter to Diana Morgan, offering both boys free places. The letter explained:

> We are a co-educational independent school with premises close to the hospital. We have only two Iraqi pupils but we are an international school where the children would be given a warm welcome. If [this is] not possible, please extend our warmest good wishes to Ali and Ahmed.

On Wednesday 1 October Ali and Ahmed visited the school for the first time. 'Our electronic entrance gates opened to reveal a huge entourage from the charity. Coming through with a stick and a smile was Ahmed, then came Ali who was very fleet of foot,' recalls Tim Hobbs, warmly. 'It was clear that they were extremely confident children, who were good humoured and happy.' They were shown around the Victorian senior school with its happy atmosphere, art and technology labs, sports hall and nice, bright paintwork. The boys started school the following morning, on a reduced day and a short week. The headmaster himself picked them up in his Lexus for the 10-minute drive to school, as he would do every morning at 8 a.m.

Mr Hobbs believed it was important for the boys to establish a base from which they could begin to integrate with the other children. He invited them to settle themselves in a converted garage with French windows overlooking the playground, where he often plays chess with pupils during lunch hour. Ali and Ahmed loved the place. They soon made friends with two boys, Pele and Michael, who helped them get around and scribed for them in biology, geography and chemistry. They also discovered that they both enjoyed trampolining – each Hall School day starts with circuit training to wake everyone up. Within a few days Ali even felt comfortable and confident enough to start teasing their jovial headmaster, who was quite unlike the teachers he had known in Baghdad. 'Pick me up in a red Ferrari will you?' Ali said teasingly each time he saw the blue Lexus. 'Ali has an extraordinary sense of humour and is very, very bright,' says Tim. 'Whenever I drive him to school, he's always telling me to honk the horn, and he's constantly pretending that Saddam Hussein's hiding around the next corner and I'd better watch out!'

A weekly routine was soon established: three days a week, Zena, from the Limbless Association, would translate for the boys at school. 'The rest of the time we all muddle along together,' says Rebecca von der Burg, the personal assistant to the headmaster, who is married to one of his original church hall pupils. 'The head is a great believer that one of the best ways for the boys to pick up English is from the other children.'

Ali and Ahmed were invited to join classes for lessons like art and maths, and design and technology. They both enjoyed music technology – and their voices were used as an atmospheric Arabic backing vocal to a CD made by the school choir. During lessons where their lack of English would be a real problem, they were given one-on-one handwriting or footwriting lessons. In some classes, such as art, they had an assistant to help them, and they also had individual games lessons to build up their balance and ball skills. There was an overarching emphasis, however, on keeping their education as mainstream as possible. 'Ali is an unusual spar to Ahmed, who has a really beautiful spirit,' says Mr Hobbs. 'At lunch Ali has a magnificent appetite. There'll be poached salmon, eggs, and a bit of *hummus* all spread on a platter before him. He regally tells Ahmed what he'd like on each mouthful.'

Both boys do a lot of sport and they were soon a familiar sight as they made their way around the school. Ali looked forward to the day he would get the second arm and would be allowed to take both arms home. He wanted to wear them to school: he wanted to look like everyone else.

On 7 October, Ali Ismaeel Abbas fulfilled the ambition of every football-mad 12-year-old when he met the most famous player in the world. The England shirt bearing David Beckham's signature had given him hope back in the dark days in hospital, following the drama of his airlift from Iraq to Kuwait. When Ali had met Sven-Goran Eriksson in September, Diana Morgan asked whether the England manager could arrange for Ali to meet his blond idol. The Football Association had phoned the very next day to suggest a meeting the following month at Arsenal's training ground before the England team's forthcoming match against Turkey.

On a beautiful autumnal day, Ali met his hero in person. 'Sven welcomed us again with that wonderful smile, and then there was Beckham and the entire England camp crowding around asking how the boys were,' says Diana who, together with Ahmed and Ali, were the only visitors allowed on the pitch that day.

One top player noticed that Ahmed was shivering with the cold and offered him his own England sweatshirt to keep warm. As for Ali, he was so overcome with the moment that he suddenly couldn't think of anything at all to say to his hero.

'He just stared wordlessly at David,' recalls Diana. 'I said, "Sorry, David, Ali seems to have become a little shy," to which David responded, "They usually do, Diana."'

The waiting press were calling for a photograph, so Diana and David herded the unlikely ensemble into a fairly chaotic grouping, before Diana asked Ali's questions of the divine David, something she didn't mind doing at all. 'Ali would like to know whether you can score a goal for peace, please, at the match against Turkey,' Diana said. 'I will do my very best, Ali,' David replied.

The Arabic translator then arrived by Ali's side, and suddenly the boy found his voice. 'I have many photos of you at home, I used to collect loads of photos of you…' he said quickly, before excitement overcame him and he ran out of words again. David smiled broadly: 'Thanks, Ali.' Then it was all over. The team jogged away to start training, while Beckham, whose thigh was strapped up, was driven back inside for a physiotherapy session. The boys watched the squad training with Sven, and were even invited to kick a few balls to David James, practising in goal. He very indulgently encouraged them, and kept kicking them back.

Ali says he will never forget that meeting, but he was yearning for something even more precious: the dream of looking like everyone else. He had found it very difficult to come to terms with having no arms by his sides. It certainly didn't feel right, and it was desperately frustrating that he could no longer look after himself, but it also just looked wrong.

In early October, using his foot, he drew a picture of Alexandra Williams. 'I was doodling in my notepad when he said, "Alex, please give me the pen; I will draw,"' she recalls. 'Clasping the pen between his toes, first he sketched me and wrote my name; then he said, "And now I draw Ali." I watched as he very seriously drew his head, body and legs. He added eyes and nose and a big smile, but I had to look away when he didn't draw any arms.'

At last the day had come. Ali's second arm, the cosmetic left arm, had finally arrived. The straps to connect it to the myo-electric arm were ready. All that was needed was the presence of one very excited 12-year-old boy. Nick Hillsdon pulled both the arms out of their plastic packaging. The myo-electric one now boasted a new, designer detail – a Manchester United tattoo that Ali had requested a few weeks earlier. The crest was printed on to a solid rectangle of plastic and had been bolted into the upper arm. Nick fitted the arms over the thick fabric of Ali's pressure-suit. First the heavy bionic one, and then the lightweight cosmetic arm. The lithium ion battery was plugged in and Fiona helped put his T-shirt back on. A large mirror was standing in the corner of the room. This was an important psychological moment in Ali's treatment: for the first time in more than six months he would be able to look in a mirror and see a reflection of himself whole.

'When I first saw my reflection in the mirror, I thought, "Look, they're mine!"' Ali recalls brightly. 'I thought no-one would be able to tell the difference.'

The new arms weren't real, but they nonetheless made perfect visual sense. Ali loved looking normal again. Uncle Mohammed's eyes brimmed with tears as he kissed the boy tenderly on the top of his head. They had been through so much together in the past six months, and now Ali finally had the arms about which he had dreamed for so long.

'I'm all here now,' Ali said confidently as the *Tonight With Trevor McDonald* camera crew recorded his elation and Alexandra took notes. 'My arms feel good,' he added triumphantly. 'I didn't think they'd look this good. I've been told they're going to look even better when they have the proper covering, it will look just like my real skin, and will even have freckles. If only my sisters could see me now. I want to hug my sisters and the rest of my family.'

From his pocket, Mohammed pulled a symbolic gift: a gold metal wristwatch that he attached wordlessly to Ali's new right wrist. 'The watch was given to me by Nafisah, Ali's Kuwaiti physiotherapist. I gave it to Ali to make him feel he'd be leading a normal life soon,' Mohammed explains.

The following day, Monday 13 October, Ali was the *Daily Mirror*'s front-page story – not for the first time. The headline captured all his joy in just four simple words: 'Ali Gets His Arms'. A large colour photograph showed Ali smiling as he wore both arms together. Aware that her regular updates on Ali were now coming to an end, Alexandra added a moving personal tribute to her page two news-story:

Ali is a remarkable and intelligent child. Some may think I am almost obliged to say that. After all, here is a severely disabled boy who has lost those closest to him. But these words are not flippant. He does not know the meaning of self-pity. And he approaches life and his treatment with a bravery that is truly humbling. As an example Ali ticked me off when we went to the circus recently. The audience was clapping but, sitting next to him, I did not like to join in. Turning to me he said in a disapproving tone: 'Are you not enjoying this, Alex? It's very good but you are not bothering to clap.' Typically, he was making his own applause by banging his feet on the ground. Mohammed, the man Ali trusts above all others, is now the boy's legal guardian. He oozes kindness. If the word luck did not sound so out of place when talking of Ali, you would use it in respect of who he has for an uncle … Ali is only at the beginning of the greatest challenge of his life. But he has already proved he has the courage to win.

But Ali's arms can never be real substitutes for those he lost, and in some ways his greatest challenge was beginning just as the media attention began to fade. 'He thinks he is very lucky to get his arms, but the next stage is going to be very difficult,' says Mohammed, with, as ever, great wisdom.

CHAPTER NINETEEN

'I Thank God a Thousand Times'

'I've got used to my situation now, but sometimes I experience some phantom sensation where my arms used to be: I sometimes feel my original fingers. It's like a ticklish feeling. It used to happen more and I got a bit weary of that. It used to happen mainly in the right arm, and a little in the left.

'Sometimes I get a bit itchy. When you can't put your hand on your back it can be hard to itch so I have to rub myself against the back of a chair or something.

'Today I have been drawing and writing with my new arm. I was competing with the teacher. I said, "You write with your left hand, and I'll write with my artificial arm, and we'll see who can do better." And I did better! She asked me to write things like, "I am clever; I am good."'

Ali Ismaeel Abbas

Another digestive biscuit shattered. Ali giggled as crumbs flew in all directions for the third time that afternoon. He was impressed by the power of this hand. 'Hmm, shortbread fingers might do it,' said Fiona.

Every day after school Ali went up to the hospital for an OT session with Fiona Carnegie. She had devised a great reward-based game to teach him how to master the simplest part of his new arm, the electronic wrist, but it was going to take a bit of refinement. The idea was to hold a biscuit with the bionic hand and then practise revolving the wrist until it correctly aligned biscuit with mouth – allowing a big bite. That was the idea, but digestives clearly weren't up to the job. Each time Fiona poked them between Ali's new fingers they crumbled as he closed his fist. Fortunately, shortbread fingers proved much more successful.

Ali had had few problems mastering his new artificial wrist. He just had to remember to make sure it was switched on, and then to pull back on the strap across his chest. Operating the electric hand was much more difficult. 'Learning to open and close the hand was a struggle,' recalls Fiona. 'Ali could get movement, but only sometimes.' Ali found this very frustrating. His challenge was to learn exactly which muscle he needed to tense to make the fingers respond, and he was finding it quite difficult to isolate the pectoral muscle beneath his armpit – the one that allows you to pull your upper arm in towards your ribcage. Instead, he kept flexing the remaining bit of bicep, which produced nothing but frustration. If the more easily controlled biceps had been chosen as the site for the electrodes, Ali's fingers would have opened whenever he moved his arm forward to flick up the elbow, but the different functions of his new arm needed separate control sites. Knowing what didn't work didn't make the process any easier, however. 'I was very eager to start practising so that I would be able to use them with ease. But it was very difficult at first and I sometimes got cross,' he remembers.

Fiona says he would withdraw at those moments, and sometimes ask to take the arm off altogether. She'd been encouraging Ali to practise opening and closing the hand by picking things up and dropping them elsewhere, but he clearly wasn't finding this much fun. How could she make it exciting for him? The answer lay, again, in Ali's favourite drink. One afternoon Fiona lined a few Coke cans up on a table. 'See if you can crush them,' she suggested. Ali opened the fingers and slid the hand around the thin aluminium. He concentrated hard and pulled his residual limb in towards his ribcage by using the muscle under his shoulder. The resulting crunching sound was a supremely satisfying aural reward. He did it again and again, laughing joyfully each time. Soon Fiona was encouraging him to pick up a can, crunch it, and then use the wrist to spin the can the other way up before dropping it off the side of the table. It was a bit like controlling the joystick on a games console.

'I was very impressed with how he easily managed to operate wrist and hand independently, and then bring them together,' says Fiona. 'Soon he could do it on demand.' She kept herself alert to any other cues and soon noticed that Ali was a child who responded well to individuals he liked. 'In one session he achieved so much in a bid to impress Alexandra Williams from the *Daily Mirror* that Fiona asked her to come again,' says Nick Hillsdon.

'When I first walked into Fiona's session, I could see a little boy talking to Fiona,' remembers Alexandra. 'I didn't have my glasses on and I was looking for Ali. Later I told my news editor that I was standing there for a moment before I realized that the little boy with the arm was Ali. He didn't believe me, but the arm just looked so natural that I didn't recognize Ali.'

Ali was overjoyed to see Alexandra, and he wanted to try brushing her hair now that he had the arm. One day he managed to carry a stool from one side of the room to the other for her to sit on. Within a few days Ali had also mastered the flexion-assist elbow. 'He actually taught himself,' recalls Fiona. 'He was running around and he flicked it up and it just locked in position. From then on he had very little difficulty with it.'

On Thursday 16 October Ali was allowed to take his new limbs home for the first time with the words of his occupational therapist Fiona Carnegie ringing in his ears. 'Try to wear them about an hour a day,' she beseeched, but Ali was much more interested in the biscuits, topped with a violent shade of dark blue icing, that he had just finished baking with his feet that day for Diana's birthday.

'Diana, Diana,' called Ali, as the charity executive popped in to the occupational therapy room a few minutes later. In his desperation to give her the birthday card he had painstakingly drawn and signed with his foot, he was hopping across the floor while holding the envelope between the toes of his right foot. His right mechanical hand had somehow got twisted back to front; Fiona ran over, spun the hand back to a more natural position and then popped Ali's card between the fingers so he could hand it to Diana himself. 'Oh, Ali. That's amazing,' said Diana, consumed by laughter and tears, as she opened the card. 'You've drawn me with one leg longer than the other!' A message, in meticulous cursive writing, said, 'To Diana, love from Ali.' The letters were surprisingly small and compact, but the wobble in each one betrayed the amount of time they had taken to write.

Within Fiona's oft-repeated entreaties lay the key to Ali's future independence: he needed to make wearing the arms a habit. Only then would they have a chance of becoming useful to him in the long term. 'They are definitely not going to be useful if he doesn't practise wearing them and using them to solve day-to-day tasks,' she says. 'Ali has to get through the phase of being frustrated with their limitations, but using them nonetheless, if he's ever going to discover that they are useful in the long term.' She had observed on many occasions how Ali was inclined to favour his feet when presented with a task. 'Being able to use both his feet and his prosthetic arms is important, but I've had to make a lot of deals with him: "Do a little bit with your arms, and then you can use your feet,"' she says.

Sitting in her swivel chair in the small office at the end of a short hospital corridor in the rehabilitation unit at Queen Mary's, a photograph of her daughter Lara, Ali's friend, near her computer, Diana looked reflective. 'Everyone has now seen Ali with his arms, and they think, "Great, he's got new arms, end of story,"' she says. 'Members of the public who aren't aware of disability issues think that once someone has their new prosthetic legs or arms or a wheelchair, that's it; but we know that it's just the beginning of a very long process. And for Ali the most difficult time of all is now as reality begins to set in. He's taking his limbs home for the first time. He knows how heavy they are and how hard and artificial they feel. He knows how the straps that keep the arms in position constrict him. For the first time he can comprehend the extent of his treatment – both its possibilities, but also its limitations; this can be a very tough few months.

'I'd imagined that my artificial legs would start where my residual limbs finished, but they don't. In my case one of them goes high up, into my groin. They are absolutely vital to me, but they are not part of me and yet they dominate my lower body. Fortunately, the staff at Roehampton are acutely aware of all of this and they very slowly help you rebuild and adapt your life.'

Zafar Khan, the equally inspirational chairman of the charity, also relates to the challenge of Ali's new arms. 'He is wearing something that is not part of his body. It is hard, it is heavy and it hurts,' he says. 'Wearing an artificial limb can be uncomfortable – it can rub on you and sores develop.' He explains that physically you are forced to develop a higher pain threshold and emotionally you begin to grieve for the life you have lost. 'Before you get your arms, you have high expectations: you allow yourself to believe you can go back to where you were. But it is only after getting your new arm or leg that you realize that actually you cannot. When I got my prosthetic leg, I thought initially that my limitations were due to lack of effort. I thought

I was holding myself back, but gradually I came to the point where I began to accept that actually I would never run or play cricket again. Slowly you begin to make compromises.' He says this degree of adjustment takes some years.

Those who have lost limbs are also forced by circumstance to forge a new identity. 'Losing a limb forces you to deal with the death of a large part of your body,' explains Diana. 'You go through a kind of bereavement for the person you were before. In my case I had been running my own company, travelling the world. I had a boyfriend, a car, a flat on the fourth floor – and overnight I felt I'd lost everything I knew.' During the first year after her accident Diana tried to defy what had happened to her by attempting to rebuild the life she'd had before: after nine months of rehabilitation she returned to her London-based public relations agency. 'The defining moment for me was hearing a PR agent moaning down the phone about the colour of a celebrity's hair.' She shudders at the memory. 'I realized then that I could no longer care, when there are people in my position all over the world.' It was a catalyst that drew her to become involved with the Limbless Association in 1995, and to become a trustee in 2001.

Ali's life has already changed immeasurably. His previous existence – that of a boy living in a small village outside Baghdad – died along with his arms. Ali survived only because his tragic circumstances coupled with his articulacy and his attractiveness marked him out for international attention. And at the moment the first camera captured his image his destiny changed forever.

When Ali arrived in England, Dr Ahmad Al-Shatti suggested, perhaps controversially, that the boy was 'a child with a mission', who had the potential to become 'an ambassador for peace'. But what if Ali should instead wish to be an ordinary man with an ordinary job? 'He can still make that choice,' insists Dr Al-Shatti, who has become a sort of unofficial godfather to Ali, visiting him every few months, talking to him regularly on the phone and offering him emotional guidance. 'Ali likes the feeling that people love and care about him, but he also recognizes that it carries a certain responsibility,' explains his garrulous and worldly patron. 'He is aware that other victims of the war are not getting the benefits of international attention that he has received. He is also a very intelligent boy, but he has a very extreme disability. I want to help him grow as a leader, rather than risk him becoming a spoiled child. This sort of guidance doesn't stop him giggling, or playing computer games and football, but it is important that he is given the opportunity – with education and supervision – to make sensible choices.'

At the end of October Ali travelled with Dr Al-Shatti to a ceremony in Hamburg, Germany, to collect from ex-Soviet president Mikhail Gorbachev a World Award that had been made to the doctors and nurses in Iraq and Kuwait for their professionalism during the war. Also receiving an award, for lifetime achievement, was Christopher Reeve, the former Superman actor who was paralysed after falling from his horse in 1995. The event made a big impression on Ali for two reasons. First, he stood on a platform in front of 1500 guests and 450 journalists and delivered a speech. 'I never thought I would be able to do that,' he says, excited by the memory. And then there was the experience of meeting Christopher Reeve himself. 'He could only move his head, and I felt very sorry for him. He was stuck in the same position. I kept asking myself, "How can he sleep? How can he eat? And what about that machine, this thing that breathes for him?" Suddenly I realized that I was OK: I can walk and I can breathe by myself. Seeing him made a big difference to me, but I feel very sorry for him. Now I thank God a thousand times that I am OK.'

CHAPTER TWENTY

A Boy with a Future

'When I wake up in the morning, I just want to put them on. I feel complete when I wear them. First, I check if there is a full battery. If it's working OK, I put it on and go to school where I write with it. Sometimes I open doors with it, but I can't use it yet to eat or drink: it's too slow. So other people help me with those things. When I come home, I take them off.

'I'd like to continue my education here, but I'd like to go back to Baghdad a lot as well. Nothing's been decided yet. I had a nice e-mail from someone in Mexico who has a similar injury to me. And he said, "Please don't give up, Ali." He said he used to work with his father (I think his father was a builder), and there was an accident and he lost both his arms. He was about 14 or 15 then. And then a charity from the US sponsored him and offered him treatment, and he's 35 now and he's got a [Masters degree] and he's getting married this year. And he said he just wanted to convey this message.

'I do miss Iraq. I want to go for a visit and then come back. I've got plenty of friends in Iraq. I would like to get back to my sisters. I love the place where I was born. I don't know about the future – just let me grow.'

Ali Ismaeel Abbas, December 2003

The atmosphere inside Ali and Ahmed's London home is warm and confiding. There is always laughter and hospitality to be found. Friends visit frequently and perch on the leather sofa suite, sipping chai, while they watch the headlines on an Arabic satellite station and chat about the news of the day. Ali's uncle Mohammed and Mohammed, Ahmed's father, take the bus into Kingston, west London, a couple of times a week and shop for groceries with which they cook fragrant meals that everyone present is invited to share, either in the smart dining room with its cream chairs protected by plastic covers, or on the low table in front of the television where they put down newspaper to protect the wooden surface from spills. Mohammed feeds Ali, and seems to take only the odd mouthful himself. His devotion to the boy is tangible.

On the walls in the sitting room, facing the garden and the golf course at the back of the house, are framed photographs of Ali's surviving family in Iraq. On the mantelpiece are the most recently received letters and cards from well-wishers. Ali has received nearly 2000 letters since he was evacuated from Iraq – each one has been personally answered by the staff of the Limbless Association. Ali and Ahmed have become exceptionally close and are constantly laughing. In the summer they played a lot of football in the garden, but their winter obsession is a Scalextric car track with Mini Cooper cars, given to them by Thomas Edwards, set up on the landing and which Ali plays with his feet.

The boys' bedroom off the first-floor landing is typically messy, with clothes and toys strewn across the floor. When Ali and Ahmed first arrived in the UK, they chose to share this room. The ground-floor bedroom that was to have been Ahmed's now contains several prayer mats. On their trip to Germany they also insisted on sharing the same room. At night, if Ali needs to go to the bathroom, he wakes up Ahmed, who assists him. 'I'm learning more and more about understanding how I can help Ali,' says Ahmed. 'It's a bit difficult to feed him with one hand. I've never fed anyone before, but I'm getting better. How has Ali changed since he's been in England? Well, he's more mature, speaks better English and has put on weight. I try to be patient and understanding.' Does he expect to be Ali's friend forever? 'If God is willing, I hope we know each other until the end of our lives.'

The children are now well known around Roehampton's Rehabilitation Centre. 'They love to play hide-and-seek, and will take any opportunity to pop out from behind a door and give you a fright,' says Diana. 'They did it to one of the workshop technicians and he was so surprised he dropped his coffee.' Whenever the boys are up at the hospital for an appointment, they always insist on visiting the charity office to say hello. 'Ali and Ahmed take great delight in mimicking us, saying "Limbless Association" (which is actually quite hard to say) quietly into our telephones,' says Diana. 'So sometimes we put them on to our more persistent callers who are always amazed to hear the boys themselves.'

Whenever Ali catches sight of one of his medical team in the hospital corridors, he always calls out. 'He and Ahmed never let me pass without being recognized,' says Dr Soori. 'I hear a shout "Doctor! Doctor!" and when I turn around there is Ali, smiling. He has no hesitation about making contact. He is very bubbly and open that way.'

Zena Al-Ugaily is also kept busy by her involvement in the charity. She was only supposed to be working part-time, and had originally contacted the Limbless Association in June with a view to helping them establish their proposed limb-fitting centres in Iraq, before she was invited to translate for the boys. Her phone now rings constantly on the boys' behalf as she arranges appointments and liaises with the school, as well as acting as an efficient and informative translator for media interviews with the household.

Diana and Zafar visit the house regularly for meetings, and once a week Diana and her daughter, Lara, come in the evening for one of the Mohammeds' delicious suppers, the children giggling at each other as they eat. 'I always say to Ali, "How's your English?" and he always responds, "How's your Arabic?"!' says Diana. Fortunately, a cleaner visits once a week to help keep the large house clean and tidy. Peter Wilson sometimes visits, so does Alexandra Williams, who says, 'I look on Ali first and foremost as a friend who I would protect, not as a story.' Ali's captivating manner has drawn together the support and friendship of an unlikely group of individuals.

On school days the boys, still hoping each morning that it will have transformed overnight into a more exciting car, are picked up by Tim Hobbs, the headmaster, in his blue Lexus. The children at Hall School have now fully accepted Ali and Ahmed. 'It's all quite normal,' says Tim Hobbs. 'They don't think, "Poor old them." Instead, they appreciate both Ali and Ahmed as incredibly nice children. They are also impressed with their dexterity in kicking a football. They've made a lot of friends.'

In October Mohammed Al-Bader, the Kuwaiti air traffic controller who had become a good friend while Ali was in Kuwait's Ibn Sina hospital, visited as he had said he would. On the day before Ali left he had made him a promise. 'He always asked to see my face without glasses and I always said no, just to tease him. On his last day in Kuwait I promised that I would take the glasses off when I visited England. Early in the morning after I arrived at Ali's home in London I awoke to the sound of giggling. Ali was standing beside me. My glasses were on the bedside table. Ali turned around and ran out of the room, laughing and yelling, "I saw his face, I saw his face!" I started to laugh and said to myself, "Finally Ali won." What I like about this bright boy is that he never gives up.'

On Sunday 26 October 2003 Ramadan began. This month of prayer, purification and fasting is the most sacred time of year for the world's one billion Muslims who are required to abstain from food, drink, smoking and marital relations during daylight hours. Their new life in the UK meant that Ali and Ahmed had to get up as early as 4 a.m. to fulfil the diktats of religious tradition: they needed to eat breakfast each day before the first weak rays of winter sunlight filtered across south London. By 2 p.m. they were exhausted and were allowed to leave school early. Once Ramadan was over, the boys began completing a full school day, before returning home for one-on-one English lessons with Zainab each evening. The boys are advancing at different rates, so at the end of September they started separate lessons. This was also a response to their constant chattering. 'Finally I had to split them up,' explains Zainab, who had been steeling herself for the moment. 'They had gone through a phase of good-natured bickering, like a husband and wife! They wouldn't listen to me at all, in the end. It was the only way to get them to pay attention.' With Ali, Zainab is now able to focus on conversational skills, while in his lessons Ahmed is learning to read and write clearly.

Headmaster Tim Hobbs looks forward to further improvements in the boys' standard of English, not least so he can understand them better. 'Ali is aware that he's in a slightly special position. He knows that he is allowed to leave the classroom or go home early if he is having difficulties. On a couple of occasions he's thought, "Blow this. I don't want to be in this class" and has gone to sit it out. Unfortunately, I'm not yet at a point where I can always tell when he's in discomfort or whether sometimes he's winding us up. Ali has also fallen over in the playground a couple of times. He can't put up his hands to protect himself and it can be a bit awkward to know how best to help him up. He's very strong-willed, and without the language it's difficult to tell when he's upset, but there is not one occasion that either Ali or Ahmed have shown any kind of trauma.'

He expects to put Ali in for an Arabic GCSE soon. 'On present performance Ali will get a lot of good GCSEs,' says Tim. 'He won't have any difficulties. He's got an extraordinary memory, he doesn't forget anything you tell him and I sense he's still holding a lot back. One day I was teaching him about multiplying fractions, which is quite complicated (particularly with the language barrier), and he wasn't applying himself, so I said, "I know you're bored. As soon as you show me you can do this, you can leave." Something that had taken half an hour was done in half a minute.'

The school has helped bring normality back into the lives of both Ali and Ahmed. 'I can't thank Tim Hobbs enough for offering them an education,' says Diana Morgan. 'Hall School has given them the chance of developing a new routine, which from my experience is exactly what you need after a trauma like this.'

When Ali was first allowed to take his arms home, Fiona Carnegie had instructed him to wear them for an hour a day. This was gradually increased to two hours, and then to four, as he became more used to them. 'The next stage is for him to wear them from 8 a.m. until 2 p.m. each day in school,' Mohammed explains. 'After Christmas, he is going to wear them all day at school. So far he is able to open a door, and use a computer.' Ali is also learning to write with them, but he can't bathe himself yet. He is hopeful that in time, with continued practice, he will master these more intricate movements. 'He understands that he is still in the practising and learning phase,' explains Mohammed.

In the future Ali will be free to decide how often he wants to wear his arms or whether he wants to wear them at all. Igor Pavlovets, the Belarussian boy who came to the UK for treatment after he was born without a right arm following radiation poisoning, has decided not to wear a prosthetic arm. But then, unlike Ali, Igor has one healthy arm. 'Ali may want to wear one arm in the future, he may want to wear two, he might not want to wear any,' says Nick Hillsdon, the prosthetic arm specialist. 'It will be for Ali to decide. He'll try lots of different types of arm in the next few years, I'm sure. I can see him wanting to wear a lightweight pair of cosmetic arms for playing football or for mucking about in, just to give him a bit of balance and so he feels he looks normal, which seems understandably important to him, I suppose, having started his life with two arms.'

It is often the parents of disabled children who encourage them to use prosthetic limbs. 'They are concerned about their child's appearance, they want to make them appear wholesome to their friends and relatives, but often, when a child grows up, they make the decision to discard them, reasoning, "If people are concerned about my appearance, it is their problem, not mine,"' says Dr Soori. 'Sometimes they start wearing them again when they begin to develop relationships with the opposite sex.'

A recent US study of amputees claimed that 50 per cent of arm patients don't wear prosthetic limbs. However, the majority of those surveyed have lost some degree of function in a single arm or hand only. In the UK a slightly higher proportion of patients wear prosthetics. 'I have one patient who only wears her prosthetic arm when she is driving,' says Nick. 'Rather than a hand it has a clip for the steering wheel.'

Such a customized approach would be available to Ali if he were to develop a particular hobby or interest in the future. A fascinating array of specialized attachments now exists for arm amputees. The chosen implement, tool or gadget is plugged directly into the wrist socket, by-passing the need for keen DIY'ers to try to hold on to pliers or a screwdriver: for taking photographs there is a useful camera holder, were Ali to develop an interest in fishing he could request a fishing-rod holder, for mastering those golf swings there is a golf appliance, and for evenings with his friends he could even select a snooker cue rest.

There is even a potato-peeler attachment for use in the kitchen. Each gadget used to be specially designed, but a wide off-the-shelf range is now available. 'We always try to fulfil everyone's needs, though, so if someone needs a little extra, we're happy to muck about and make it for them,' says Nick.

Ali's scars are healing well, and within the next couple of years their angry purple colour will fade until they blend in with the rest of his skin. They are already much more elastic, which means it is easier for Ali to move around. When he returns to school after the Christmas break, in January 2004, Ali will wear his arms for the entire school day.

He has found great comfort in having two hands at the ends of his sleeves, but although he has now made great progress in mastering the functionality of the arms, he sometimes chooses to switch the hand and wrist off. It also turned out that he wasn't particularly interested in the silicone 'glove', which mimics real skin, that Nick Hillsdon showed him in November. Intricately painted and detailed, it fits snugly over the pink plastic arms, but it does make Ali's hands seem a bit too large for his body. 'The fingers look a bit too much like sausages with the silicone glove bulking them up. We might have another go, but Ali really wasn't that bothered either way by the silicone,' says Nick. 'Function for him now seems more important than appearance.'

Ali recently delighted in demonstrating how he can now use his arm when he and Ahmed met two young Iraqi patients who have arrived for prosthetic limb treatment as wards of the United Arab Emirates. And in a recent television interview, while Nick was talking about the technical challenges of Ali's arm, Ali impishly switched the hand on and sat sweetly while it revolved around and around and around.

Just after this book goes to press, Ali will undergo a review in which he will be offered a second myo-electric limb to replace his cosmetic left arm. 'We've already discussed the idea with Ali, and he seems keen,' says Nick. 'He's tolerated the weight [1.5

kilograms] of the existing electric arm well, so we would make him a similar socket for the left arm, which would help to spread the load over his extensive scar tissue. Quite often we start patients with a lightweight arm before building up to a more functional limb.'

If Ali does receive his new left arm, it is most likely to have the same flick-up-and-lock elbow as his right arm, as well as an electric hand. Where it will differ is in not having wrist rotation: 'You need rotation in the hand you use to eat, but this arm will have a simpler function as a carrying handle,' Nick explains. Chris Garwood has a similar set-up – with one fully functioning arm and one with partial function.

While Ali is still growing, the prosthetists at Roehampton intend to build new sockets for his arms every two to three years. Nick expects he will be ready to receive a larger hand when he is 15 or 16. He also expects Ali to benefit from advances in artificial arm technology. 'By the time Ali is in his early twenties I hope he will be able to operate his hand and arm by electronic signals direct from the brain rather than the muscle,' Nick says. 'This would allow him to think the word "open" and the hand would respond.' Ali Abbas could become, quite literally, the bionic man.

And if he so wanted, he would also have the opportunity to try split hooks – like Chris Garwood's – in place of cosmetic hands. The third, fourth and fifth fingers on Ali's hand have no electric function, and can make it more difficult to operate the single grip between thumb and first two fingers. Split hooks allow a greater degree of fine control. 'By the time he is 16 or 17 he'll know what he wants,' says Nick. 'He might want a pair of electric arms and a pair of sports arms. He might want one electric arm only, or no arms, or split hooks. Only time will tell.'

Although rehabilitation at Roehampton is patient led, Fiona Carnegie nurses private hopes that Ali will retain his commitment to using his new limbs. She is particularly keen to see Ali learn to feed and dress himself, but concedes that there are cultural issues to consider here. 'In British culture we prize independence, but I constantly have to remind myself that Ali comes from a country where people expect to look after each other. There is a different emphasis.' From January 2004 onwards she expects to see Ali every three months, extending after several sessions to once every six months. 'I want Ali to continue to have choices. I want him to know that I will be there to assist him if he chooses increased independence in the future.'

He would no doubt benefit from the wisdom of her counsel. Dr Soori and his team feel confident that Ali has a good chance of being able to lead an independent life if he wants it. 'Ali has the intelligence, motivation and determination to do well,' says Dr Soori, who expects that he will also benefit from future advances in voice-activation technology, whether he persists with his arms, or not. 'It is clear that he will find it laborious to write, so a voice-activated computer would be a real benefit with his studies, as would a Dictaphone.' And by the time Ali is a young adult, he could have his home custom-fitted with a hands-free system to control his environment. By the time he is a young, independent adult he should be able to adjust the television, heating and lighting in his home, control the oven, and open and close doors, and curtains, by speaking commands aloud to a central processor.

Before that, however, Ali's fourteenth birthday – on 9 February 2005 – will bring another form of liberation. Ali will finally be allowed to remove the restrictive pressure garment that he will have worn for two years, in a bid to restrict the flow of blood away from the scar tissue. Hopefully his scars will then lie flat and smooth upon his skin.

On 1 December Mohammed received a very moving phone call. 'He got the news that his wife has had that baby,' says Ali, excitedly. 'They have called the baby Ismaeel, after my father!

One of my sisters, Isma'a, had a baby girl in July and she called her Azhar – after my mother. Now I'm an uncle twice! Maybe my uncle's boy will marry my sister's baby one day, and it will be another Azhar and Ismaeel – just like my parents were.' He rolls around on the carpet giggling at such an attractive idea, and of course, in Iraqi culture where intermarriage between distant cousins is very familiar this is not such an improbable suggestion.

The date 1 December was also significant for another reason: Ali painted his first picture using his artificial hand rather than his foot. His school art teacher, Brenda Steward, was very proud of this masterpiece: a bold picture of a London bus heading towards a very brightly coloured traffic light. The bus is neatly outlined in black paint, as are the windows. The body work is bright red, the windows dark blue.

A few days later Ali spoke on the phone to his stepmother, Layla. Mohammed overheard the conversation with his sister, 'For the first time Ali called her "Mum",' says Mohammed. Following the destruction of Ali's home, Mohammed's sister Layla moved with her children, Ali's half-sisters and his half-brother into Mohammed's house. This house is not large, so with two large families living there it is now a tight squeeze. The Kuwaiti government has offered to fund the purchase of a new property in Za'Faraniya as part of its commitment to Ali's family – or perhaps the family will choose to build a new dwelling on the land that Ali's parents saved so hard to buy.

Ali's future has been endlessly debated since he came to the UK in August 2003. Initially, both boys' treatment here was to last six months, but as the weeks passed and both Ali and Ahmed settled down in the UK this date began to seem unrealistic. It now seems hopeful that Ali will remain in the UK indefinitely. Tim Hobbs has offered both boys places for as long as they want them.

'Ali understands that with Iraq in turmoil his future lies in Britain,' says Dr Al-Shatti. 'If he leaves now, he will be forgotten, but if he returns to Iraq with a qualification it will make a big difference to his future. A child responds to the expectations of his environment – staying to be educated in the UK will provide him with a goal.' The Limbless Association is hopeful that residency visas will be issued in due course. This will, of course, have significant implications for Mohammed and his family. Mohammed has committed himself to Ali's care, but still yearns for a way to resolve his personal heartache at his separation from his much-loved wife and children, and now his new baby boy.

'I would love to return home to Iraq, yes, but I am aware that Ali has much better opportunities here,' says Mohammed, who, as the boy's legal guardian, is now committed to him as a parent. 'Life is complicated because I am also responsible for my family in Iraq. I can only pray that there is a way for us to all be together, so that we could overwhelm Ali with our love, and watch him grow to independence. Having his family around would complete him. I'm praying to God for a way to deal with this; but, no, I will never leave Ali: he has no-one else.'

These are absolutely remarkable sacrifices to contemplate making. Why would a man give up so much for a boy who is not his own? 'He's a child that is alone now,' says Mohammed. 'I am responsible for him. I have a duty to stand by him and guide him into the future. The only way he can make his future happen is with firm and loving guidance. He has lost two parents, but he still has so much left. I'm with him, he has a stepmother, and a brother and sisters. Since I've been in England I've seen people with worse disabilities make successful lives: I believe that Ali has a good chance of being at least as successful as they have been. I could never take the pain he has been through. He has tolerated so much, yet if I get so much as a scratch I am barely able to handle it. Yet I have watched him coping every single day. Ali is one courageous boy. I pray to God not to let our hopes for Ali's future drift away. This is an exceptional boy.'

Mohammed has already done so much to support the 12-year-old during his darkest moments, and in the process he has given Ali a new sense of belonging. Throughout their shared ordeal, his quiet wisdom and gentle, affectionate nature have also provided Ali with a profound example of how to be a man. On 10 December Ali Abbas was honoured with the International Child of Courage medal at the thirtieth *Woman's Own* Children of Courage Awards, in a beautiful service at Westminster Abbey. When he was asked before the starry event which British celebrity he would most like to present him with his medal (the congregation included numerous television personalities), Ali replied without hesitation. 'Lara – she's my biggest star.' He had chosen an unknown 10-year-old, the daughter of the Limbless Association's chief executive, Diana Morgan. Ali has many challenges – and no doubt some suffering – to come, but the beauty of his spirit remains undiminished.

Many see in Ali an inspiring symbol and, yes, in some ways Ali is a symbol: of courage and resilience at the personal level, and of reconciliation and peace at the collective one.

But his friend Catherine Ecolivet, the French missionary, has words of wisdom for us all. 'I prefer to see a little boy – sorry, Ali – a young boy, who laughs and spends a great deal of time teasing people with the complicity of Ahmed. It is a good sign: they are kids.

'Yes, I will always remember the wounded angel who landed in my life on a quiet spring evening. But today, for me, Ali is a very human boy – a brave heart, a valiant soul and a living miracle.'

EPILOGUE

January 2004

During the eight months since Saddam Hussein's five-tonne bronze statue was dragged from its plinth on 9 April 2003, Iraqi citizens like Mohammed and Ali remained haunted by the disappearance of the dictator that it represented. They felt a combination of fear and utter hatred for Saddam, and were terrified that he would one day be restored to tyranny. 'It's like one of those horror movies where you think the villain is dead but then he suddenly jumps out at you,' says Mohammed.

On Saturday 13 December 2003, their anxieties were eradicated when the cowering 66-year-old dictator was captured alive by a 600-strong US strike team as he crouched in a cramped dugout – barely larger than a grave – a few miles from his home town of Tikrit. He was pulled ignobly from his lair beneath a polystyrene hatch disguised as a rock, where he had been breathing through a crude ventilation pipe pushed into the mud. In bombastic eve-of-war speeches he had urged his people to fight to their deaths, yet he gave himself up without firing a single shot from his own pistol.

The following day, after DNA tests had confirmed the prisoner's identity, crowds took to the streets in Baghdad, music played from balconies, cars honked their horns and jubilant gunmen fired celebratory shots into the air (injuring at least 26 people). When artfully demeaning footage of the heavily-bearded fallen dictator being medically examined after his capture was broadcast at the official coalition news conference on Sunday, the Iraqi journalists present couldn't contain themselves. They leapt to their feet, jubilantly punching the air.

The regime that had terrorized Ali's family and many millions like them, was at an end. Mohammed embraced Ali, who was dancing around the room with a giggling Ahmed as the family heard the news on Sunday morning. 'Saddam is Father Christmas!' said Ali, laughing. 'And not only because of his big, white beard. He's also given me a very, very big Christmas present. Now I can look forward to a peaceful Iraq in years to come. For the first time I feel that my country has a future.'

It was the best welcome-home gift he could have received.

Ali Ismaeel Abbas hadn't seen his youngest siblings since the night a missile devastated their lives. They had said goodnight to him and when they awoke a few hours later they were covered in rubble, their father was dead and Ali had gone. The older relatives who had tended Ali while he lay in agony in a Baghdad hospital had doubted whether he would survive. Now he wanted desperately to be reunited with them. 'I wanted to go back to Iraq for all the things I love there,' says Ali. 'My family, my friends, the land I was born in, the games I wanted to play.' In early November, he spoke the words he could no longer contain. Diana Morgan recalls, 'We'd all had a lovely day together and at the end of it Ali said, "Please, Diana, please, Baghdad for Christmas." His wish to be reunited with his surviving family was a very strong and very positive instinct, and I understood exactly why he wanted to go back; he feels so far removed from his family and he wants to share with them all the nice things that have happened to him. But I was also aware that the visit would raise a lot of painful feelings. When I myself went home for the first time, having lost both my legs, reality struck me very hard, so I said to Ali, "You must go home, of course, but do not be too worried if you get very upset indeed – that's a very natural way to feel." I thought he might brush off my remarks, but actually he became very thoughtful.'

Before leaving England, Ali confided in his English tutor, Zainab Hashim. 'He used to say, "How am I going to go back to Baghdad, and cope with all the wailing?" In the UK he is used to being surrounded by limbless people and to everyone else being quite calm about his disability but he knew that, in Iraq, people's emotions are displayed more visibly. The thought of what he would have to face made him quite upset. My heart was really feeling for him when he left.'

Ali, Ahmed and the two Mohammeds flew to Kuwait City, en-route to Baghdad, on Tuesday 16 December 2003, just three days after Saddam's capture. They took with them boxes of presents for their families, including a tiny illuminating Christmas tree that Mohammed said he would like to give to his wife, Shatha. During the flight to Kuwait City both boys were invited up to the cockpit by the Kuwaiti pilot, Saad Alhazaia, who told the cabin crew to take care of Ali 'who is like our son'. Awaiting the party on the tarmac at Kuwait International Airport were representatives of the Kuwait and American military, as well as Mohammed Al-Bader, the jovial air traffic controller, who invited them to stay at his house for the next few days.

It was imperative that Ali's return to Iraq was conducted in an atmosphere of secrecy. His international profile created the risk, in a country struggling to find its equilibrium, that Ali could be kidnapped and held to ransom. For this reason, no-one other than his closest friends and family were told about his first trip home.

'Lawless elements in Iraq might wrongly think he is bringing a lot of money with him, therefore it is vital that Ali's visit is kept low-profile for the safety of all the group,' Dr Al-Shatti explained. 'For that reason, most of the transportation will take place at night, and family gatherings will be conducted in private.' Furthermore, a number of military planes and helicopters had recently been shot down in Iraqi airspace. Yes, I am worried but I believe the Alliance will take every precaution. 'I believe that the emotional advantages to Ali in being reunited with his family far outweigh the risks. He has a lot of ideas and challenges inside him, and it will be very valuable for him to compare his current situation with what he has left behind, even the small things. I spoke with him about how he would react to not having 24-hour electricity or being able to have a bath or shower with ease.'

During their stay in Kuwait City, Ali and Ahmed were reunited with old friends, including the French missionary Catherine Ecolivet. They also had lunch with Nafisah Kamal, Ali's devoted former physiotherapist, 'I showed her how I can write holding a pen in my new hand and she was so pleased,' says Ali, and at Ibn Sina Hospital they visited the medical team to thank them for skilfully nursing them back to health, and to show them their new prosthetic limbs. One member of the physiotherapy team, Robert, kissed both the boys' new artificial hands, an act of huge respect in Arabic culture. Finally Ali proudly received the money he had earned from the cards printed with his paintings, and announced that he would give a percentage to Ahmed and his sisters.

Throughout his brief holiday in Kuwait, Ali's mind was preoccupied with thoughts of his return home to Baghdad at the end of the week. 'Before I went back I was tense,' he says. 'I kept asking myself, "How am I going to cope meeting my family again?"'

Ali's uncle Mohammed was also nursing concerns. 'I felt I needed to go to Iraq, I wanted to see my wife and my babies again, and there were so many things that needed to be sorted out. At the same time I was afraid that if we travelled by land we would be looted or kidnapped. Fortunately, when we arrived in Kuwait, we were told that we would be going by plane.' A Kuwaiti officer, Tariq Al-Doseri, had been put in charge of a small team of military personnel responsible for returning the party safely by US transport plane to an airbase in Baghdad on Friday 19 December 2003. It was exactly 248 days since Ali had left Iraq, uncertain whether he would survive to set foot there again.

'The big plane made a very scary noise and plunged around the sky to avoid any missiles. Then we went to my aunty's house in Za'Faraniya. Everyone was there and they were all crying with joy, and so was I. I really couldn't believe my eyes or that I was with them again. It was like a dream for me, it didn't seem real. They said, "Hello Ali" – they were as happy to see me as I was to see them. We had lots and lots and lots of cuddles. It was just lovely there. They were also happy to see that I've got arms. They said, "Congratulations Ali!" Mama Layla [Ali's step-mother] was very happy to see me, she kept bringing me lovely food. Every now and then she gave me a kiss and she arranged a very nice mattress for me to sleep on. I wore the arms the first day, but just before I went to sleep I took them off. I asked my little sister Hadeel to sleep in the bed with me and I asked her to scratch my back, just like she always did. I used to have to bribe her to do it, but now she does it for free.'

Ali Ismaeel Abbas, January 2004

The journey from the air base to Za'Faraniya, the town near the demolished village of Arab Al-Khrsa where Ali grew up, was complicated by the need for the group to travel in secret. The plan, arranged by telephone from Kuwait, had been for Mohammed's brother-in-law to meet the party at the airbase with a hired minibus at 11.30 a.m. Unfortunately, the group was held up by paperwork and he was turned away by an American security guard, alert to suicide bombers. Finally, just before

4 p.m., their Kuwaiti chaperones drove the group to a Baghdad taxi rank. By the time the innocuous-looking taxi-bus they had hired arrived at Ali's aunt's house in Za'Faraniya, Mohammed's brother-in-law was frantic with worry, and the boys were starving. Someone went to collect Ahmed's family from their home as plates of delicious-smelling, crispy roast chicken were placed by Ali's aunt on the wooden table.

'Just as we were about to take a big bite, the door burst open and all our relatives came in,' recalls Mohammed, laughing. 'Everyone was there: children, elderly aunts, and they all wanted Ali to go home and stay with them.' Mohammed was overjoyed to see his wife and to meet his beautiful new baby boy, Ismaeel, named after Ali's late father. He gently cradled the swaddled infant and stroked his soft black hair.

'Everyone was jumping around me then, saying, "Come and stay in our house,"' says Ali. 'I decided to go with Uncle Taha.' Taha's house had taken the impact of the stray missile; his wife Kameela had been killed, as had three of his five children and nine members of his wife's family. Taha proudly told Ali that while Ali had been in Kuwait and England he had rebuilt the house himself, bigger and better than before. And it would soon become home to Ali's sisters who had decided to live with Taha's surviving family. Furthermore, Taha's son Mustafa and Ali's sister Hana'a had decided to marry when the year of mourning is past.

All of Ali's enthusiasm evaporated the moment he arrived at the patch of land beside a single-track road beneath a row of date palms overlooking the river. What had once been a lively community of small houses was now a wasteland. The rubble of destroyed houses had been cleared away by bulldozer, and rising out of the bleak, muddy ground, like a monument to positive thought, was Taha's new house. The grey concrete façade was depressing enough, so was the knowledge that the remains of the bomb had been buried just a few feet away near an open sewer, but what hurt Ali most of all was the sight of a small section of breezeblock wall, painted blue, that had been left standing between Taha's house and the road: part of his family's old lean-to bathroom, surrounded by a sea of fragments that had slipped through the bulldozer's wide teeth. The last time Ali had stood on this spot he had been running inside to go to bed. There had been a vegetable patch, cows and a busy community of family and friends. It had been his whole life. Now he felt as if he was looking at a tombstone.

'I was very sad when I went to that place,' says Ali sombrely. 'I lost my family and my friends there; they were in that house when the missile fell. When I saw the rubble I couldn't bear it, I started to cry and I couldn't stop.' One consolation was the appearance of Rio, Ali's black-and-white dog, who still continues to hang around the bomb-site, existing on scraps, despite the disappearance of his family. He ran towards the sobbing child wagging his tail.

After half an hour, Ali had had enough. 'I want to go back to my uncle's house, I don't want to stay here,' he cried as Kareem Jassim Ahmed, a neighbour and father-of-six whose house was the only one in Arab Al-Khrsa left standing after the missile strike, steered him towards the comforting embrace of Mohammed. 'He looks fine, doesn't he,' said Kareem as the men shook hands. 'That took plenty of effort from us, I can tell you,' replied Ali's uncle.

Seeing Ali healthy and well was particularly moving for 44-year-old Kareem. A few days later, Mohammed spoke to this modest hero about the night he rescued a young boy called Ali Ismaeel Abbas from the devastation of his home. As Kareem spoke, this thickset gentle giant sat cross-legged on a rug, drinking chai.

'At 11.55 p.m. I heard bombs falling. I put my family into an air-raid shelter I had built. I then went straightaway to Ali's house because I saw fire and people gathered there. I tried to put out the fire with water then I went inside and saw Ali's father was dead, I went to leave but I heard Ali shouting, "I'm here". He was covered in bricks and blocks in the bedroom. His legs were under an eiderdown in the burning room. I picked up Ali and his hand fell off: his arms were melting, just like candles. I cried when I saw him. I took him to a clearing on the water's edge and then to the car belonging to another neighbour, Mohammed Al-Jambi, who took him to hospital. Afterwards we went and started removing the dead bodies. Some of them were in pieces. There was a loose wire on the ground and it threw me backwards, I have a scar on my shin where I got repeated electric shocks from it. I was so sad for what happened to Ali's father and the rest of his family: Ismaeel wasn't killed by the rubble but by the fire. We were neighbours since the 1950s and now the village has gone. Ali is changed, but I was relieved to see that his health came back. I wish him well.'

Meanwhile, Ali was wrestling with complicated emotions. He had wanted to visit his parents' graves at the shrine of Abu Arrooge, but was dissuaded by Mohammed, who thought it would be too much for him to cope with. Instead, like any healthy 12-year-old, he spent most of his time at home playing; he taught his sisters tricks to win on the PlayStation he had brought them, and he kicked around a football with his cousins, on the few occasions he could be coaxed outside. He would wear the new limbs only in front of his immediate family.

'When he was in Baghdad, Ali was self-conscious about his appearance,' says Mohammed. 'In Britain and Kuwait people have only known him without arms, so he can relax, but his family knew him when he was whole. He showed them how he could eat an orange and some rice, but after that the sisters decided to spoil him and do everything for him. My services were dispensed with! His sisters preferred him to wear the arms, but it was clear that they were hoping that Ali would be able to do more with them. They did not realise how long it takes to learn to use them. I explained to them that he is still at the practising and training stage, and told them not to give up hope.'

Ali is an emotionally aware child and he sensed that his family were struggling at times with his new appearance, particularly the youngest children who had not seen him since the day before the bombing when he had two natural arms, just like them. 'When they saw me they were always happy, but I sensed they were uncomfortable and didn't want to show it. I think that they were dealing with their feelings in private,' he says with great perspicacity. But, despite these undercurrents, being with his family filled him with joy.

Leaving them again, on 14 January 2004, was unbearable. 'I was crying a lot to say goodbye,' Ali says. On the morning of his departure, in the midst of organising four *bulbul* (Iraqi singing birds) for Nafisah, and several beaten copper plates for the Prime Minister of Kuwait, Ali turned to Mohammed with tears in his eyes. 'I'm not going, I'm staying,' he said, beginning to cry. 'We reasoned with him, and reminded him of the importance of his new life,' says Mohammed. 'But he still cried all the way back to Kuwait, and for days afterwards.'

Ali, Ahmed and the two Mohammeds stayed in Kuwait for a week, where Sheikh Sabah Al-Ahmed Al-Sabah, the Prime Minister of Kuwait, hosted a reception on the party's return, before returning to the UK on 21 January. Mohammed says, 'When we first came back to London Ali was crying for his friends and for his family. He kept asking me, 'When do we go back to Iraq?', so I called his tutor, Zainab, and she brought some Iraqi boys around to play with him. She took him to the movies, and gradually he is forgetting how sad he felt.'

Ali and Ahmed returned to Hall School after their extraordinary, extended Christmas holiday on January 27th.

'I want to stay in Baghdad with my family, but I know that living in London is the right course of action because of my treatment and my education. I want to thank my uncle for leaving his family to care for me here. Crying won't help: it won't get me things back. I'd better get on with it and get my education. I'm thinking now of becoming a computer engineer, it's something I can do. But after I'm trained I will be going back to my country and I will be visiting a lot between now and then. The situation there is much better than it was. When I was in Baghdad the other day, I was visited by my old teachers. They used to beat me, but they love me now! One of them, my English teacher, has been visiting my sisters and weeping while I was in London. So I said, "Now that Saddam has gone do you still stand up in school and say, 'Long live Saddam'?" And the reply was, "No, we don't do that now. Now we say, 'Long live the people, long live Islam'." There is still violence in Baghdad, but it feels safer now. The war is good and bad. It is good because the tyrant has gone, but it is bad because it hit innocent people.'

Ali Ismaeel Abbas, January 2004.

One must say Yes to life and embrace it wherever it is found – and it is found in terrible places ... For nothing is fixed, forever and forever and forever, it is not fixed; the earth is always shifting, the light is always changing, the sea does not cease to grind down rock. Generations do not cease to be born, and we are responsible to them because we are the only witnesses they have. The sea rises, the light fails, lovers cling to each other, and children cling to us. The moment we cease to hold each other, the moment we break faith with one another, the sea engulfs us and the light goes out.

James Baldwin

SPECIAL AFTERWORD BY

Mohammed Abd Hamza Al-Sultani

I would like to dedicate special thanks to the media people who told what was happening and got Ali out of Baghdad and to Kuwait. We consider the British and Australian media to be the main reason why Ali's life was saved. However, without the heroism of Kareem Jassim Ahmed, who pulled Ali from the flames, he would not have had a chance. We are grateful to Fatin, his nurse in Baghdad and the first voice to bring attention to Ali's situation, as well as to the military personnel and medical staff who helped evacuate Ali from Iraq.

We want to thank Sheikh Sabah for facilitating Ali's arrival in Kuwait, for treating Ali like one of his own sons, and for paying for Ali's treatment in Kuwait and the UK. We thank the Limbless Association for their hard work, and Diana Morgan for leading the team; we thank Zafar Khan for giving Ali his first hope for the future and bringing us to Britain. We thank all the medical staff in Baghdad and Kuwait, as well as the medical team in the UK who have given Ali his new limbs and taught him how to use them. We have so many friends, many of whom have helped us from afar, in the US, India, Canada, France, Australia and many other countries, and we thank you also for the many cards, letters, teddy bears, gifts and donations you have sent. Thomas Edwards, Eman Mustafa, Catherine Ecolivet, Um Abdulla and Samiha Ayoub have been particularly supportive friends to us, as has Mohammed Al-Bader who welcomed us into his home in Kuwait and looked after us even though he was also needed by his family at the time. We are grateful to Zena Al-Ugaily, Zainab Hashim and the Iraqi volunteers who help us by attending appointments, and to the headmaster, Timothy Hobbs, who offered Ali and Ahmed places at Hall School in Wimbledon. They take good care of the boys and treat them exceptionally well. We appreciate the support of the Kuwaiti health office who are in regular contact with us. They always ask if we are okay, and update us on plans for the future. Dr Ahmad Al-Shatti has been a particular friend to us and has followed Ali's story from the beginning. I would also like to thank Mr Ian Mackay of the immigration department at the Home Office for his care and concern in dealing with our case. Finally I would like to thank Caroline Spellman MP, the British ambassador to Kuwait, the President of the Canary Islands and the other diplomats and politicians who have supported us.

بِسۡمِ ٱللَّهِ ٱلرَّحۡمَٰنِ ٱلرَّحِيمِ ١ ٱلۡحَمۡدُ لِلَّهِ رَبِّ ٱلۡعَٰلَمِينَ ٢ ٱلرَّحۡمَٰنِ ٱلرَّحِيمِ ٣ مَٰلِكِ يَوۡمِ ٱلدِّينِ ٤ إِيَّاكَ نَعۡبُدُ وَإِيَّاكَ نَسۡتَعِينُ ٥ ٱهۡدِنَا ٱلصِّرَٰطَ ٱلۡمُسۡتَقِيمَ ٦ صِرَٰطَ ٱلَّذِينَ أَنۡعَمۡتَ عَلَيۡهِمۡ غَيۡرِ ٱلۡمَغۡضُوبِ عَلَيۡهِمۡ وَلَا ٱلضَّآلِّينَ ٧

In the name of Allah, most gracious, most merciful
Praise be to Allah, the Cherisher and Sustainer of the worlds;
Most gracious, most merciful;
Master of the Day of Judgment.
Thee do we worship, and Thine aid we seek.
Guide us on the straight way,
The way of those on whom Thou hast bestowed Thy Grace;
Not of those who earn Thine anger nor of those who go astray.

How to Help

The Limbless Association is the national UK charity for amputees and people with congenital limb absence. The Association provides information, advice and support for people of all ages who live without one or more limbs. It has a nationwide network of volunteer visitors who are all amputees themselves, offering support and encouragement to prospective amputees, carers and those already trying to come to terms with limb loss or deficiency.

In April 2003 the Limbless Association launched the ALI Fund (Ali's Fund for the Limbless of Iraq) in response to Ali Abbas's plea in the Baghdad Hospital for 'new arms'. This fund is currently covering the continual care and rehabilitation of Ali, Ahmed and their guardians, while they stay in London.

Ali is just one of many Iraqi citizens whose lives have been devastated by war. The Limbless Association is committed to helping others who have also lost their limbs in Iraq. If you would like to make a donation to help with this work, please do so in the following ways:

By cheque:
The ALI Fund
Limbless Association
At Roehampton Rehabilitation Centre

Roehampton Lane
London SW15 5PR

By credit card:
0208 788 1777 (office hours 0900–1700)
We accept all major cards except American Express (Amex)

By direct donation:
Account Name: The ALI Fund – Limbless Association
Account number: 00796833
Sort Code: 30-96-88

If you would like to make a personal donation to Ali's Trust account:
The Ali Abbas Settlement Account:
Account Number: 32329964
HSBC
Poultry and Princes Street
London EC2P 2BX

Further Reading

Chong, Denise, *The Girl in the Picture: The Remarkable Story of Vietnam's Most Famous Casualty* (Simon & Schuster, 2000)

Cockburn, Andrew, and Cockburn, Patrick, *Out of the Ashes: The Resurrection of Saddam Hussein* (HarperCollins, 2000)

Lewis, Bernard, *The Middle East: 2000 Years of History from the Rise of Christianity to the Present Day* (Phoenix, 2001)

Macmillan, Margaret, *Peacemakers: The Paris Peace Conference of 1919 and its Attempt to End War* (John Murray, 2001)

Mount, Ferdinand, *The Theatre of Politics* (Shocken Books, 1972)

Sasson, Jean, *Mayada – Daughter of Iraq: One Woman's Survival in Saddam Hussein's Torture Jail* (Doubleday, 2003)

Wilson, Peter, *A Long Drive through a Short War* (Hardie Grant, 2004)

Zangana, Haifa, *Through the Vast Halls of Memory* (Hourglass, 1990)